THE COMPLIANCE MAZE

A GUIDEBOOK EXPLAINING THE LAWS AND REGULATIONS THAT GOVERN CALIFORNIA PUBLIC TRANSIT OPERATORS

MICHAEL L. STANGE

THE COMPLIANCE MAZE

A GUIDEBOOK EXPLAINING THE LAWS AND REGULATIONS THAT GOVERN CALIFORNIA PUBLIC TRANSIT OPERATORS

Michael L. Stange

Published by:
Always in Compliance
16025 Perry Heights Drive
Riverside, California 92504

Cover Design and Interior Graphics by Gwendolyn Rhodes

Copyediting and Book Interior Design by Lynette M. Smith

First Edition

Disclaimer

This guidebook is intended to provide a general understanding of commercial vehicle laws and regulations that govern California public transit operators. And while the book includes much of the commercial law relative to compliance and other "Matters Regulated" and the inspection/audit process, it is in no way representative of the exhaustive legal reference documents which are fully contained in the California Vehicle Code, Title 13 California Code of Regulation, *Title 49 Code of Federal Regulations*, The Commercial Vehicle Safety Alliance North American Standard Out-of-Service Guide *and the* National Fire Protection Association Codes 10 and 52.

Any challenge to a legal reference in this book to include what constitutes an Out-of-Service condition or an Unsatisfactory inspection or Terminal Rating shall be ultimately determined by the reference documents and/or the CHP Motor Carrier Safety Unit assigned to an agency.

Further, commercial vehicle laws and regulations are subject to change often and without notice. Subscribing to updates for Title 13 of the California Code of Regulation *and purchasing new Commercial Vehicle Safety Alliance, National Fire Protection Association,* California Vehicle Code, *and applicable Federal Codes (referenced in the book) are strongly recommended.*

Contents

Figures

Preface

"I've Worked in Public Transportation for 30 Years. Why Should I Read This Book?"

The purpose of this book is to provide essential compliance information to public transit service providers, individuals responsible for regulatory compliance, and anyone involved with local, state, and/or federal compliance inspections and Terminal audits. The information identifies requirements and guidelines necessary to obtain Satisfactory administrative and Terminal inspection Ratings, explains how the law affects your operation, and gives you the critical tools to present legal-based information from a position of knowledge and authority.

The truth is, most transit personnel cannot explain the fundamentals of a compliance audit based on the language of the law, the difference between a law and a regulation, and the regulatory factors that affect their business from equipment Out-of-Service criteria to driver requirements, record retention, and other Matters Regulated. This book provides all that information and much more, while citing legal requirements by reference document and section. And regarding the understanding of commercial vehicle law, don't allow yourself or others to believe that the legal requirements at your agency are properly monitored and thoroughly understood. Unfortunately and undoubtedly, few transit personnel have ever read the compliance reference books that govern maintenance programs, driver requirements, or the CHP compliance audits and other required inspections.

There is much to be learned from the reference documents, applying the regulations and by establishing an interactive relationship with the CHP Motor Carrier Team outside of audits, which is the beginning of developing a fact-based compliance program(s) that will improve your organization by grounding it on commercial vehicle law.

I'm certain this book will challenge transit staff, new and veteran alike, to read the reference documents not through foggy goggles but through spotless prescription reading glasses. And then I've been told, with a reserved sense of pride, by many transit managers that their CHP audits are always Rated Satisfactory. In essence, they're saying that "status quo" is acceptable and reassuring to them and that the current program(s) are serving the intended purpose. To quote General Colin Powell (Retired), Joint Chiefs of Staff,

Too often, change is stifled by people who cling to familiar turfs and job descriptions. One reason that even large organizations wither is that managers won't challenge old, comfortable ways of doing things. But real leaders understand that, nowadays, every one of our jobs is becoming obsolete.

Public transit professionals throughout the nation are tasked with the monumental responsibility of putting bus service on the road every day of the year for their valued customers. The equipment is required to be safe, reliable, well maintained, and properly documented, while the drivers must be competent, be thoroughly trained, and possess a current commercial driver license, endorsement, and medical certificate. Equally important, their Hours-of-Service time must always comply with the requirement of the law as cited in *Title 13 of the California Code of Regulation* §1212, Article 3, under General Driving Requirements.

Unfortunately, many individuals within the transit industry have not received regulatory compliance training or are not familiar with the applicable laws and regulations that govern their actions or the organization. Therefore some have struggled with understanding and more importantly applying the regulations and components of the CHP Terminal audit and other required administrative reviews and inspections. What truly sets transit professionals apart is the ability to accurately defend their programs according to law, explain how the regulations correspond with state and federal law, and manage their compliance program.

What affects specific departments for compliance, ultimately affects the entire agency in many ways. For example, buses are removed from service for unsafe conditions, Terminals are subjected to audit by the CHP, and state money is released upon the Satisfactory Rating of Pull-Notice and the Drug and Alcohol inspections.

During my 39-year career with the Los Angeles County Metropolitan Transportation Authority and interacting with many transit professionals nationwide, it is apparent that the industry would greatly benefit from a single-source guidebook such as this, which explains the laws, regulations, codes, and alliances that govern the public transportation business. The book exposes the regulations, explains the document "adoption" practice, and highlights essential information that will greatly help many employees, whether represented or non-represented or from lower- to senior-level personnel within the organization.

Understanding regulatory compliance is a necessary part of the business, and yet the compliance effort can be challenging, at best; without adequate information and training, serious mistakes can and will be made. And if you want to "red line" your patience meter, do not attempt to maneuver through the copious laws and regulations applicable to commercial vehicle operators without the miracle ingredient of appropriate information, guidance, proper training, and a willingness to embrace an attitude of learning.

The individuals who would benefit the most from reading this book include Maintenance Mechanics, drivers, supervisors, managers, or anyone involved in

CHP Terminal and required administrative reviews. Senior management should, at a minimum, become familiar with the information in the book, resist the temptation to "read it later," and make available to themselves the legal reference documents listed in Chapter 5.

I cannot overemphasize that middle and senior management take a more active role in communicating the requirements of commercial vehicle law, familiarize themselves with this book, and initiate a close relationship with the CHP, which is a valuable resource although not readily available to provide training. If asked about commercial vehicle instruction, CHP personnel will most likely refer you to their Programs and Services Department, which provides commercial industry education for the commercial vehicle operator. And since the final Terminal or administrative inspection Rating ultimately resides with upper management, they must possess at least a foundational understanding of the law, especially if the agency has struggled through audits.

All too often, upper management is preoccupied with myriad agency issues while the demands of managing the organization often prevent them from being closely involved with on-going regulatory issues. This book provides a basic understanding of the law, discusses who is or should be responsible for regulatory compliance oversite, and explains the annual CHP Terminal inspection procedure. More importantly, the information within these pages provides a clear understanding of the status of the agency's programs relative to the language of the law, which should eliminate any surprises upon inspection.

Not only should a transit agency always be prepared for Terminal and administrative audits; the fleet, driver status, and records should be accurate and available for presentation within 24 hours for bus crashes, for unannounced inspections, and/or for legal reviews by law enforcement, the CHP Multidisciplinary Accident Investigation Team, or mandated bus legal holds.

Whether you're a veteran transit employee or a new hire, I hope I've presented clear and valid reasons that compel you to read this book. And I trust, for your benefit, that I've made a persuasive and compelling case; because the greatest respect you can give a Terminal or an administrative inspection that has been Rated Unsatisfactory is fear, and fear is the thief of peace. Believe me, some Maintenance/Transportation and administrative managers, directors, and others responsible for regulatory compliance who unfortunately have experienced an Unsatisfactory Rating, in some cases, have made that mistake only once!

Some contract service providers have explicit language in their contracts regarding bus pull-out/cancelled service, Terminal inspection Ratings, regulatory compliance violations, and other Matters Regulated that can and in some instances do invoke liquidated damages and that may possibly affect the fate of their careers.

"Why should I read this book?" asks the 30-year transit veteran? I say, don't fall prey to complacency or mediocrity. To quote Colin Powell once again, "Even the pros have leveled out in terms of their learning and skills. Sometimes even the pros can become complacent and lazy." Thirty years in any business does not guarantee continued success unless you work hard, remain focused, and discipline yourself in staying current with the laws and regulations that govern your agency.

Read the book, apply the information, work closely with your CHP Motor Carrier Team, and strive to become a valued regulatory compliance expert.

Foreword

Progress and a Need for Regulatory Compliance

From horse and cable-car conveyance systems of transportation in the mid-1870s to high-tech alternative-fueled and electric-powered buses, public transit is meeting the challenge of operating efficiently and effectively utilizing modern innovations while constantly seeking new ways to improve vehicle safety, enhance ride quality, and provide greater mobility. System improvement, ridership growth, trip afford-ability, and a desire to provide excellent service are among the transits' top priorities.

In no other profession do so few improve the lives of so many than in the public transportation industry. Each day, countless millions of Americans throughout the nation arrive at and leave their destinations on safe, clean, comfortable, and reliable buses.

The decision to use public transportation is a personal choice, and such decisions are as varied as the cities and towns across the nation. Notwithstanding, buses provide a viable option for many who do not have access to a car, want to reduce the stress of driving the congested roadways, choose not to use a car, or cannot use different forms of transportation. Advanced-design transit buses of today are comfortable and reliable; they electronically announce destination stops, accommodate wheelchair patrons as required by the Americans with Disability Act, "kneel" to allow easy front door access, and much more. And now, many buses throughout the country offer Wi-Fi capability.

Along with advanced technology and modernization, however, comes the demanding responsibility of ensuring the equipment is not just safe but compliant according to state and federal commercial vehicle law and Out-of-Service criteria; and that the driver meets strict requirements regarding Hours-of-Service regulations, training, endorsements, and other compliance factors. Regulatory compliance is critical to ensure that commercial vehicles operating in revenue service are properly maintained according to law and that driver requirements are not compromised, thereby reducing the number of truck- and bus-related collisions on the roadways. In addition, California state law requires the CHP, Motor Carrier Safety Unit (MCSU), to inspect buses, driver regulations, and administrative programs for compliance. They will Rate the agency's vehicle maintenance program, inspect the status of records management, and determine that drivers maintain current commercial vehicle driver licenses and medical certificates, receive the required transit training, and have proper endorsements.

The information provided in this guidebook will help you understand and more easily navigate the maze of laws, regulations, and codes that govern their equipment, driver regulations, and other programs.

Further, the book is complete with necessary regulatory information that all levels of staff in public transportation need to know; specifically for the Maintenance and Transportation Departments and for those responsible for managing the Department of Motor Vehicles (DMV) Pull-Notice and/or Drug and Alcohol Programs.

The Boy Scouts of America motto is "Be prepared." As a public transit mechanic, driver, supervisor, instructor, manager/director, or executive professional, are you prepared and qualified to explain your regulatory compliance program to law enforcement, legal entities, and/or attorneys? Do the records at your agency reflect the true and accurate condition of the equipment? Are all drivers with a CDL trained according to the requirements of the law? And are the Pull-Notice and Drug and Alcohol Programs current and accurate? Last, do you have immediate access to the proper reference documents that govern Terminal Inspections, Non-Revenue, Pull-Notice and the Drug and Alcohol Programs, and proper vehicle maintenance?

Remember, a foundational understanding of commercial vehicle law and regulations is required of most all transit personnel to ensure that the regulated programs are safe, reliable, and compliant at all times. Commercial Vehicle Regulatory Compliance for transit fleets is not an option, it's essential—because that's the law!

Terminology and Legal References

The key to understanding regulatory compliance words and terms and to effectively apply their use resides in learning proper terminology and references. Most professions tend to use and unknowingly develop specialized jargon, reference words and unique phrases that, for the most part, are common and generally appropriate for the business. The California Highway Patrol, Motor Carrier Specialists, the legal community, and law enforcement use such words, phrases, and verbiage as well, while citing federal and state law, codes, and the Commercial Vehicle Safety Alliance when working with California public transit agencies and their staff.

This book is replete with unique words, phrases, and legal references for reasons of introducing, to the fullest extent possible, the world of commercial vehicle law and regulatory compliance, as told in the proper (industry) vernacular for the learning experience. As such, it is necessary to begin building a new vocabulary that will allow you to effectively communicate with compliance and regulatory enforcement and oversight entities. Most of the words and terms have critical meanings exclusive to the public transit business, primarily within the Maintenance and Transportation departments. And without a foundational knowledge of the language, you may not fully understand the implication as to how it may impact your Terminal inspections and administrative reviews. Therefore, the use of standard industry words is intentional, since the same words and terms are generally referenced and/or cited by law enforcement, motor carrier specialists, and attorneys, as well as throughout the commercial vehicle enforcement business.

The book cites, where applicable, the appropriate reference documents and sections for quick access, review, application, and study purposes. And though much of the regulatory language may initially seem foreign, you will quickly gain the confidence to "speak the language" and use it to your benefit and advantage without having to rely on others.

Last, for your learning edification and simply to prevent you from becoming confused with similar terms, reference titles, and words presented throughout the book, below I have explained the different references/clarification for frequently used words and terms.

For example:

1. The document that addresses Out-of-Service violations for a commercial vehicle is known as the CVSA, which stands for Commercial Vehicle Safety Alliance. Yet on the cover of the document it is referenced as the *North American Standard Out-of-*

Service Criteria Handbook and Pictorial. For purpose of discussion, it's acceptable practice in the industry to refer to the document, with the CHP or any official entity as the CVSA, the Out-of-Service Guide, the *North American Standard,* or even the Out-of-Service Criteria. The foregoing references allude to the same reference document and are clearly understood throughout the business.

2. The resource document most often referenced for general commercial vehicle information regarding motor vehicles within the state of California is the *California Code of Regulation, Title 13.* The document is often referred to as the CCR, Title 13, 13 CCR, or by its full title, *Title 13 California Code of Regulation.*

The "13" is only an identifying number issued for the title which designates Motor Vehicles. There are 28 different California Code of Regulation titles from Environmental Protection to Military, Veterans Affairs, and others. Of the many California Regulations, this book exclusively references Title 13, Motor Vehicles.

3. *Title 49 Code of Federal Regulations (Transportation)* is the full title; however, it is commonly referred to as 49 CFR; or, simply, if you're discussing a transportation issue and you know the "Part," it can be referred simply as the Federal Code or by the Part.

Before continuing, be aware of the frequently used miscellaneous words and terms that are used interchangeably throughout the book and by public transit operators, enforcement professionals, and legal entities that use and convey the words differently. Some of the commonly used words and terms share similar meanings throughout the commercial vehicle industry, the CHP, and law enforcement, and it's important to know them.

Here are some of the common words or terms loosely used throughout the book, which have the same or similar meaning:

- Law, regulation, code, and alliance
- Audit, review, inspection
- Out-of-Service bus, dead bus, red tag bus, a hold bus
- Motor Carrier Specialist, Motor Carrier Inspector, or MCS, often referred to as simply the CHP, even though the MCS is a separate department within the Department of the CHP
- Pull-Notice Program, Employer Pull Notice, PNP, Driver License Monitoring System
- Terminal inspection, Terminal audit, the yearly audit, the annual inspection, or the safety compliance review
- Basic Inspection of Terminal, most often referred to simply as BIT
- Out-of-Service Guide, the CVSA, or the North American Standard
- CA Number, Carrier Identification Number
- Bus division, station, depot
- Agency, company, authority, carrier
- Pre-Trip inspection, Driver Vehicle Inspection Report
- Operation, agency, or company

During my career I've had the honor and privilege to work with many exceptional transit professionals who have invested their time and energy to improve and advance public transportation for countless millions of people who use the service.

Through their hard work and commitment to serve the public, they have unknowingly imparted valuable information to me throughout the years. It is they who gave me the inspiration and intellectual knowledge to write this book. My hope is that it will be used as a valuable source of information, an effective guide; a helpful tool for those who want to enhance their knowledge of commercial vehicle law and to improve their agency's regulatory compliance status and preparedness.

1

Introduction

After a 39-year career in the public transportation industry with the Los Angeles County Metropolitan Transportation Authority and having worked with many transit agencies, I am convinced of the following. Public transportation employees are some of the hardest working people I have known. Most are highly motivated, intelligent, keenly focused on providing quality bus service, and committed to the development of a company/customer relationship. They continuously strive to provide safe, clean, and reliable transportation and work hard to offer an enhanced ride experience for the general public.

Having shared my perception, I would be remiss not to say there is a considerable need in the industry for many transit personnel to better understand the rules and regulations that govern the equipment, general driver requirements, Pull-Notice Program, recordkeeping requirements, bus inspection programs, Drug and Alcohol Program, Triennial review and other Matters Regulated. Further, it is equally fair to say that most bus public transit personnel have only a vague understanding of the necessary legal documents, reference books, and commercial vehicle law that govern their agencies. Most are unfamiliar with how to properly use the different documents and don't know how to apply the law and regulations as a necessary tool to prepare for inspections or work with regulatory and commercial vehicle law enforcement personnel during accident investigations and required Terminal inspections. Understanding the fundamentals of commercial vehicle law and how to apply them is at best challenging without proper training or the necessary information from a book such as this.

For those and other reasons I have written this guidebook to introduce, in one clear and relevant document, the regulatory pillars of responsibility by specific department; compliance requirements, regardless of inspection type; and departmental regulatory responsibilities as referenced in Appendix A.

The book explains the anatomy of CHP inspections, cites vital reference documents by title and section, and explains the critical steps necessary to understand commercial vehicle law for the prevention of crashes and injuries due to equipment/mechanical defects, violations of driver regulations, and the misuse of drugs and alcohol. Further, it explains the inspection safety items of a Terminal review, which will help you begin, in a more methodical way, to understand the regulatory maze; and this will, in time, help your agency to become a more responsible and compliant organization. To that end, most of the general compliance regulations are necessary in order to understand when working with the California Highway Patrol (CHP), law enforcement, regulatory agencies, Multidisciplinary Accident Investigation Team (MAIT), attorneys, and other enforcement officials.

Therefore, roll up your sleeves and prepare your mind for action because you're about to embark upon an adventure into the world of commercial vehicle law and regulatory compliance. It's a journey that will lead many of you on a learning expedition that I suspect you've probably never experienced. The book will provide technical answers to compliance questions and give you the necessary information to connect the regulatory dots, and it will provide you with the knowledge to adeptly review your technical and administrative regulatory programs. Ancillary benefits include making you a more valuable asset to the agency, as well as helping you minimize operational risk and assisting you in determining the current performance status of the Maintenance, Transportation and administrative programs required by state and federal motor carrier law.

The United States Department of Transportation remains committed and laser focused on transportation safety and on reducing or preventing the occurrence of death, crashes, and injuries on local, state, and federal highways and throughout the entire national roadway system. It is equally committed to the California public transit (bus) operators who safely provide millions of daily passenger trips throughout the country. And though the information contained in this book is primarily for California public transit operators, all commercial motor carriers are required to maintain safe and compliant equipment, accurate driver Hours-of-Service, and an accurate records-management program.

As such, a vague understanding of the law or marginal knowledge of Matters Regulated is no excuse for improperly maintained vehicles, records that do not reflect the true condition of the equipment, improper driver Hours-of-Service documentation, or a program that does not reflect the requirements of the law, regulation, or Code. Failure to be fully compliant at all times with applicable rules and regulations will greatly expose your agency during CHP annual safety inspections, federal Triennial audits, and/or matters involving investigation and litigation!

All too often, news reporters cover the devastation that occurs when commercial vehicles—often involving transit buses—are involved in crashes resulting in fatalities, serious injury, fire, or the destruction of property. Frequently, crash events occur unnecessarily when the carrier operates equipment outside the compliance parameters of the law or when the application of Out-of-Service conditions is not thoroughly understood or properly managed. Also, driver Hours-of-Service under *Title 13, California Code of Regulation,* §1212–1215 (General Driving Requirements) regulations must be fully compliant and managed through a driver license monitoring program, otherwise referred to as the Pull-Notice Program, which is discussed in detail within this book.

To that end, safety must always be the number one priority of any motor carrier operator—especially of buses, since the valued commodity transported is human.

Unfortunately, and for many reasons discussed later, the concept and application of regulatory compliance at most agencies is not fully understood and may not exist as a definitive, fully cultivated, and established operational function. The harsh truth is that many transit professionals are less than knowledgeable regarding the laws and regulations that govern vehicle compliance, driver requirements, record retention, and other Matters Regulated. Further, most do not fully understand the CHP safety compliance Terminal inspection process and Rating methodology. Often, staff is regularly trained on new bus/equipment technology, management principals, the bargaining agreement, or some other discipline that aims to improve the efficiency and quality of bus service; but seldom are they trained on the regulatory issues that require them to be compliant against a state or federal law or regulation.

Sadly, a foundational understanding of regulatory compliance and the law never seems important until an Unsatisfactory compliance Rating is issued by the CHP Motor Carrier team or a vehicle is being held by law enforcement or the CHP for its involvement in a crash that resulted in numerous injuries or fatalities. With blinding speed, the motivation and urgency for compliance soars in importance! Like your worst nightmare come true, the mind performs quick mental gymnastics, hoping the vehicle was properly maintained and that all compliance specifics were managed and the preventative maintenance program and driving requirements were current and properly documented. If not, it's far too late to ponder the safety and condition of the vehicle, driver status, or overall status of the Maintenance/Transportation compliance and driver programs.

As such, an effective and well-planned maintenance and driver program, united with compliance oversight, must work synchronously every day, without exception. Complacency with programs and a false sense of assurance, especially within your Maintenance and Transportation departments, regarding regulatory compliance is an unforgiving foe that will, in time, fail you and your agency if not properly managed. Unlike the old adage, the things you don't know *will* hurt you.

Remember, a Terminal can be rated Unsatisfactory for various reasons or for deficiencies in any one area, as I discuss later in the book, within the inspection process. Having 25% of the equipment inspected and determined to be Out-of-Service for mechanical issues is problematic. Driver Hours-of-Service requirements (logbook time) are critical, and Maintenance/Transportation department records must reflect the true and accurate condition of the equipment and driver status at all times. Regardless, at the conclusion of the inspection, the Terminal will receive one Rating. (See Figure 1 in Chapter 6.) And if the Rating is Unsatisfactory, a re-inspection of the Terminal will occur within 120 days. Unfortunately, without a thorough understanding of Matters Regulated and without a

Compliance Champion(s) to lead the recovery effort, wasted labor hours will be expended and the desired outcome may not occur quickly enough, depending on the number and seriousness of the bus Out-of-Service violations or other violations noted by the inspector(s).

Simply, a weak or poor understanding of regulatory law is unacceptable; and if a Terminal or administrative review is Rated Unsatisfactory, unfavorable consequences will most likely occur. It may have immediate and draconian consequences, depending on the policy of the transit agency or the contract service provider. Some service providers are subject to liquidated damages or immediate staff terminations for unfavorable Ratings. Either way, explaining an Unsatisfactory Rating to the CEO and/or the Board of Directors will probably ruin your perfectly wonderful transit day.

Other required annual and Basic inspections include the Pull-Notice Program, the Triennial Audit (once every 3 years), Drug and Alcohol Program inspection, and the Basic Inspection of Terminal (BIT), all of which are discussed in the book.

Unfortunately, most transit supervisors, managers, directors, and upper-management personnel have received inadequate or no training in commercial vehicle law or the Terminal Rating process as related to compliance because, well, it has not been available and few, if anyone, at the agencies have gained appropriate knowledge to develop foundational compliance programs that are well understood and managed. Most often, the attitude was or is, "If it's a compliance issue, let the division manager assume the responsibility."

And if the attitude is "No problem, we've been consistently rated Satisfactory," the Maintenance and Transportation programs are therefore assumed effective. Careers have ended abruptly within Terminals that have been Rated Unsatisfactory. At a minimum, work life takes on a different hue for Division Managers who experience unfavorable complications with BIT, Pull-Notice, Terminal inspection and/or Drug and Alcohol Programs. And without proper knowledge of the requirements, they often struggle trying to effectively develop an improvement plan in preparation for the 120-day re-inspection.

The Department of the California Highway Patrol

The Department of the California Highway Patrol (CHP) is one of the largest police agencies in the United States. It is responsible for a wide range of duties performed, as the seven points on their officers' badges signify: Character, Integrity, Knowledge, Judgment, Honor, Loyalty, and Courtesy. The CHP enforces traffic and commercial vehicle laws and regulations on all public road and highway systems throughout the state. However, its primary role is with Transportation, involving many types of motor and commercial vehicles. The CHP also has enforcement responsibility and authority for "all roads and all codes" throughout California.

CHP officers enforce the *California Vehicle Code* and other state and federal regulations, the Commercial Vehicle Safety Alliance, and codes. They provide assistance to municipal law enforcement agencies, perform and/or assist in crash investigations, perform vehicle collision reconstruction, and conduct multi-disciplinary accident investigations and analysis for major crash events.

To aid in understanding commercial vehicle law, it is necessary to discuss the enforcement power and responsibilities the CHP possesses, since it is responsible for all commercial vehicle enforcement, vested through the authority of the California state legislature. Further, the CHP and other special responsibility teams under its jurisdiction play an active part in the public transit bus operator compliance programs for inspection requirement, enforcement of transit-related programs that are Rated for the condition of their fleet, record maintenance, general driver requirements, and other Matters Regulated. The CHP's authority is cited in the *California Vehicle Code* (CVC) §34500 Required Regulations: "The department shall regulate the safe operation of the following vehicles." The "following vehicles" is a listing of commercial motor vehicles subject to inspection by the Department giving them the authority through the state legislature.

The Compliance Maze was written for many reasons, among them, to introduce and explain, within one complete text, commercial vehicle laws and regulations that govern the public transit operator. Equally important is the need, before understanding the law, to become familiar with the CHP and its special teams responsible for the enforcement and inspection of compliance audits for the commercial vehicle operator, crash investigations, and the CHP's involvement with equipment and driver complaints.

Contrary to what many transit people think, Terminal inspection and program audits are *not* performed by CHP law enforcement officers, unless they are properly trained as Commercial Vehicle Motor Carrier Specialists (MCS). CHP officers are sworn peace officers who are authorized through the state of California to carry a weapon, detain individuals, carry out arrests, and perform many law enforcement duties except commercial vehicle compliance enforcement. Sworn CHP officers properly trained as MCS inspectors are authorized to carry a weapon and perform the duties and responsibilities of law enforcement person- nel; they are properly trained to enforce commercial vehicle law, inspect equipment as cited in CVC §34500, and render vehicles Out-of-Service for safety violations or for other related compliance issues. Sworn CHP officers who are MCS trained can often be seen on the state highways driving black and white trucks with a camper type shell, sporting the CHP emblem (shield) on the doors. And yes, they possess the authority to uphold the laws for all general driving infractions for motor and commercial vehicles alike.

If your bus is involved in a crash, the responding law enforcement agency representatives will perform their required duties; however, unless properly trained, they will not perform dynamic testing to determine vehicle speed and stopping distance, perform accident recon- struction, investigate driver Hours-of-Service status, or access the mechanical condition of the brakes or vehicle components. Local police departments, depending on size, may have a commercial enforcement division and may use them to inspect the vehicle on scene, hold the vehicle for inspection, or request assistance from the CHP to provide those services. Further, it is not uncommon for the bus, depending on the condition of the vehicle, to be either driven or towed back to the assigned facility, pending some form of inspection action. Occasionally, the law enforcement or CHP officer in charge at the scene may decide to have the vehicle sent to a designated facility other than from its home location. If the vehicle is driven to a location, regardless of the site, it can be released only by a qualified individual who has inspected the vehicle on scene and has determined it is safe, based on *Title 13 California Code of Regulation* §1230 (b) Damaged Vehicle, to be moved.

If the vehicle is driven or towed to your facility and if your agency has personnel with the proper knowledge of vehicle safety compliance inspections and who possess a good understanding of the *Commercial Vehicle Safety Alliance* (CVSA) *Out-of-Service Criteria*, often they will be asked to perform the inspection under observation of the enforcement officer or a CHP Motor Carrier Specialist. If the vehicle or bus is severely damaged or was engulfed in a major fire, especially if there were fatalities, I strongly recommend it be red-tagged, covered, and isolated from the general public and agency personnel, pending an investigation and before any repairs are made.

Last, if the vehicle is impounded by law enforcement, regardless of the extent of damage, do not move the vehicle, initiate repairs, or allow anyone to inspect it without the express authorization of the agency that placed it on hold. If the vehicle is handled without authorization while on hold, it may be determined that the evidence has been contaminated. Destruction of evidence is not a good thing, and some people will get very angry! The head of the Maintenance or Transportation department responsible for the staging of the vehicle must closely manage and properly communicate to senior management its status on a regular basis. The agency representative should work closely with the lead law enforcement agency, reminding them weekly of the hold status. Transits value their assets and want or need the equipment released so repairs, unless totaled, can quickly begin. Law enforcement agencies are busy and may, if not regularly reminded, forget the vehicle is on hold. As such, regular reminders for a vehicle release will serve you well.

Another CHP department is the Multidisciplinary Accident Investigation Team (MAIT). The MAIT specializes in detailed investigations and analysis of major traffic collisions that may have resulted in fatalities and/or serious multiple injuries. Often they perform accident reconstruction and may study the factors that could have contributed to the crash. MAIT members are well trained in commercial vehicle compliance, crash scene investigation, collision analysis, scene photography, vehicle dynamics, and other disciplines relative to motor and commercial vehicle crashes.

MAITs are strategically located throughout California in Redding, Sacramento, Fresno, Vallejo, Los Angeles, San Luis Obispo, San Bernardino, and San Diego. The teams typically consist of a CHP team leader, a few CHP officers, a Motor Carrier Specialist I, and a Caltrans Engineer. MAITs are dispatched to a wide variety of crash scenes and may perform either the full on-scene investigation or a limited investigation, depending on the nature of the event and how they are directed. Their crash investigations, accident reconstruction reports, and physical evidence, including photographs, have been used in courts of law, for arbitrations, and for other legal activities.

If your agency has experienced a major crash and the MAIT responds or is continuing with an investigation that may include vehicle inspection(s), I strongly recommend that a representative from your agency be assigned to work closely with them throughout the entire process. If assigned to assist the MAIT, the person should be familiar with the mechanics of a vehicle or bus, possess some knowledge of commercial vehicle law, have a pleasant disposition, and be capable of making good decisions on behalf of the agency.

During some aspect of the investigation, the MAIT will request information such as equipment records, driver status of duty, and CDL status/expiration to include medical certificate, endorsements, and other related information. An agency's direct involvement with the investigation will speed the process, keep the agency directly involved/informed, and give the assigned person a unique opportunity to work with and learn many things from a professional accident investigation team. It will be a rare learning experience—one that cannot be easily bought or offered through a seminar or educational program—to observe and participate in the inspection and testing of bus systems by professionals.

It is also important to understand there is no single method, manual, or correct protocol used regarding commercial vehicle response, vehicle inspection, crash event, or required activity. The important thing to know is that commercial vehicles are regulated and are governed by commercial vehicle law, setting them apart from automobiles and other rolling equipment. Further, regulated commercial vehicles require a different skill set and knowledge base. They require the understanding of commercial vehicle law, crash scene investigation responsibility, and vehicle periodic and planned maintenance programs, inspection cycle, driver Hours-of-Service requirements, and the Terminal inspection process—all of which are required by state and/or federal law.

All of the above functions are performed by either the CHP or one of its special responsibility teams under the Department of the California Highway Patrol.

Other required inspections are the Pull-Notice, Basic Inspection of Terminal (if required), and the Drug and Alcohol Program. Again, unlike what some may think, the referenced inspections are *not* performed by CHP officers, but rather by MCS personnel who are another special team under the Department of the CHP. MCSs are not sworn officers, are not authorized to carry a weapon, and do not possess the authority to detain or arrest. They will inspect your regulated equipment, records, and programs and may, at the request of the MAIT or other law enforcement agencies, perform an equipment inspection on a bus or vehicle that has been involved in a crash or unusual event.

Occasionally a commercial vehicle/bus is reported to the CHP as allegedly experiencing equipment failure, emitting an unusual noise, or having a safety-related problem or some other perceived safety issue. That type of report is generally registered with the CHP local office, but it is typically forwarded to an MCS III, who will initiate some form of investigation. The MCS III is the senior-level Motor Carrier Specialist responsible for the duty and assignments of the MCS I's and II's.

The public transits and contract service providers, especially for the smaller transit agencies, should expect an MCS I to perform most all Terminal, BIT, and administrative inspections. The MCS is knowledgeable about and well trained on commercial vehicle law, is a resource for information, and may offer some training during inspections. And unless you monitor the Federal Register for changes to commercial vehicle law, the MCS is your conduit for any and all new regulations that apply to vehicle status, driver requirements, records, or any other compliance regulation.

Commercial Vehicle Law for the Public Transit Operator

Last year, I had finished teaching the Commercial Vehicle Regulatory Compliance program to a group of transit professionals in Northern California when a woman responsible for the Pull-Notice Program (also known as either the Employer Pull-Notice or the Driver License Monitoring System) approached me. She said that not only did she consider the training informational, but it made her reconsider how important her position was. She said that when she became responsible for the program she received very little training and none of it was based on the requirements of the law. The Pull-Notice Program is cited in the *California Vehicle Code* §1808.1 Employer Notification and is discussed later in the book.

While I was teaching that component of the program, she became extremely focused and was staring at me as though hearing the information for the first time. Somewhat perplexed, she asked what legal document and section she could reference to find the Pull-Notice requirements. I quickly realized that although she was performing the duties of the position, she was clueless about legal implications, which document to reference, and the requirements to manage the program.

Sadly, she is just one example of many who are very serious about their jobs and equally enthusiastic about their individual performance in the transit business but are not properly trained to thoroughly perform the duties and responsibilities within a compliance-based job classification. She told me there were no reference documents to access, and she did not know that a Satisfactory Pull-Notice Rating was one of the requirements for the release of annual (programmed) state transportation funds for her agency. Further, she stated she was only marginally involved in the annual Pull-Notice inspection performed by the CHP Motor Carrier Team. No wonder she had a completely different perspective about her job function and responsibilities after learning about the legal implications of Pull-Notice and how it plays a vital role in the overall compliance expectation at her company. She was pleased to know the Pull-Notice requirement is easily found in the *California Vehicle Code* and assured me it would be on her desk within a week.

Unfortunately that's a common scenario happening at many transit agencies each day. Typically, individuals in more senior capacities responsible for departments that must comply with CHP-required inspections for ensuring commercial vehicle compliance, whether they understand the language of the law or not, have received minimal training, if any, and are left to their own devices to ensure that the equipment is properly maintained, that it's safe according to the Out-of-Service criteria, and that the driver requirements are satisfied. Many individuals, such as the woman I just mentioned, cannot cite the laws and regulations that govern the specifics of the business which is under their control and responsibility! And guess what: If the annual Pull-Notice inspection goes the "southern route," who do you think will be held accountable for the Unsatisfactory Rating because of a non-compliant program? Right again: She will!

If your organization does not have a regulatory Compliance Champion(s) or well-defined and properly understood compliance program(s), then I recommend that someone with authority make a decision to take immediate and appropriate action to initiate the development of one or more regulatory Compliance Coordinator(s), acquire the reference documents discussed in Chapter 5, read this book, and arrange for staff to receive some level of regulatory compliance training. It would be dangerous to rely upon your instincts as a guide or to assume that all Matters Regulated at your agency regarding vehicle maintenance, proper records retention, and the general driver requirements are compliant and that administrative audits are always ready for inspection.

The difficult questions for you or anyone else in "regulated" based departments to ask is this: Do you realize what's at risk in receiving an Unsatisfactory Terminal or administrative review? Are compliance laws and regulations properly understood by you or appropriate staff? Can you endure the burden of being cross-examined on the witness stand, based on legal challenges of your Maintenance or Transportation programs? And can you defend your department's regulatory compliance readiness against the requirements of commercial vehicle law?

Test your knowledge and that of others within your agency whom you rely on to manage your compliance activities and who are directly/indirectly responsible for the overall Maintenance and Transportation programs, record retention by law, and the Pull-Notice and Drug and Alcohol Programs. If most of the following standard questions cannot be correctly answered, then I strongly suggest that this guidebook be read *with bold intent* and that you learn and apply this valuable information. Good luck!

1. What is the difference between a short- and long-standing commercial vehicle defect?
2. What are 49 CFR and 13 CCR?
3. Where would you find the General Driving Requirements for a bus driver?
4. Does 13 CCR adopt CVSA? And what is CVSA?
5. Where would you find the criteria for a bus Out-of-Service condition?

6. After how many hours of on-duty time must a bus driver generate a logbook (grid graph)?

7. What is VTT? Where would you find the authority cited?

8. What is a Pull-Notice?

9. Why is secondary employment significant for a transit bus driver?

10. What is the 8/80 rule?

Find the answers at the end of this chapter.

Don't wait for a troublesome compliance inspection or assume your programs are and will remain Satisfactory, because a false sense of security is a difficult master to serve. Start the development process, take the time to get it right, exercise patience, and, depending on your effort, within a short time you will have a comprehensive compliance program that will satisfactorily serve your agency. Unfortunate but true: Most transit employees who are responsible for Rated programs possess only a fraction of the necessary compliance knowledge required to withstand a direct challenge or series of tough questions by regulatory professionals. If you didn't take the test, I encourage you to do so; and then ask yourself if you or others are currently prepared to engage compliance officers and inspection reviews and to defend your current program(s) from a legal challenge. And let's stop guessing about the language of the law! If you or any member of your team does not know where to find the appropriate answers to compliance questions, or does not know the differences between the reference documents, don't guess! It's easier and much wiser to say "I don't know" than to appear naïve and inexperienced.

Connecting the commercial vehicle regulatory dots and attempting to make sense of state and federal laws and regulations can be challenging without proper training. Fortunately, a J.D. degree is not necessary to understand commercial vehicle law as it relates to the public transit operator. With the information in this book, a basic reference library, and a resolve to educate yourself and staff on the language and intent of the law, the lines of regulatory communication will be free from distortion and regulatory clarity will prevail.

For the above and other reasons, this book has never been so relevant for public transit employees. From mechanic and bus driver to senior management, a good working knowledge of commercial vehicle law is necessary. More importantly, with advanced bus technology and ever-changing regulations, a newfound and clear understanding must be the order of business to better manage commercial vehicle compliance and application of the requirements. Unlike ever before, where there was almost no effort to understand applicable law, management must make a conscious decision to embrace related training and develop a compliance program for the Matters Regulated.

The book will introduce, explain, and cite the proper authority as required for compliance of all California public transits. The following reference documents by title and section are thoroughly covered: *Title 13 California Code of Regulation, Commercial Vehicle Safety Alliance Out-of-Service Criteria Guide, Title 49 Code of*

Federal Regulations (varying parts), *California Vehicle Code,* and the *National Fire Protection Association Codes 10 and 52. (See Appendix B for the front cover of each of the reference documents.)*

Key components of the regulations that require full compliance by an agency are discussed in detail, citing proper authority with a thorough explanation of the requirement and how to reference related language by document, title, and section. The book explains how to connect the regulatory dots, with emphasis on inter-pretation of compliance gleaned from the references and their application for the California public transit operator. Further, detailed information is also pre-sented regarding the necessary development of a cooperative relationship with regulatory agencies like the California Highway Patrol Motor Carrier Team, Triennial audit inspectors, and local jurisdictions that may place a legal hold on your bus or non-revenue vehicle.

Last, the goal of this book is to present clear and relevant information about commercial vehicle law as it applies directly to the public transit operator, to educate transit personnel on applicable law and regula-tions, to simplify the compliance maze, and to provide information on how to develop a team of knowledge-able Compliance Champions. No transit agency can afford to ignore the significance and necessity of having well-trained staff who understand the law and are capable of working with regulatory entities, law enforcement agencies, and legal councilors.

As I write this chapter, I can't help but think how necessary it is for the transit community to embrace and apply these regulations and to raise up the new generation of employees who should thoroughly understand compliance as the cornerstone of their business and possibly their careers. This information should be acquired, not through osmosis or the archaic "on-the-job training" method of years gone by, but rather through quality instruction, application, and support from upper management to learn and apply the law. This book is just the beginning to understanding compliance and the "new and required way" method. And before it's too late, regulatory training and program support must be encouraged by the old timers who ushered in Detroit Diesel Electronic Controls, electronic fare boxes, Advanced Design Buses, and the 121 braking systems.

If you understand the technology I just referenced, then you are at or near retirement and, I believe, obligated to encourage the new generation to learn and apply commercial vehicle law, to ensure safe and reliable vehicles and compliant programs that are inspected and Rated on regular intervals. Further, the new transit generation can be supported by preparing them for their future. This includes training on commercial vehicle law, having them work with the CHP during audits, and enforcing the need to absorb this information.

Members of this generation are smart and quick to learn, and they appear ready to embrace new challenges, regardless of technology or complex administrative/ legal requirements. And I strongly recommend that those who become the "go-to people" for compliance-related recommendations and answers not withhold the coveted and valuable legal information found in the reference documents discussed in this book. Let me illustrate what I just said with a short story.

Many years ago, as the Senior Mechanical Instructor for the Southern California Rapid Transit District in Los Angeles, I was involved in a bus procurement with the Director of Equipment Engineering. New to bus buys, I had no alternative but to rely on the director for information and assistance as we started the project. During and throughout the procurement, I noticed a rather large book about four inches thick, either under his arm or on his desk, which he would often reference or discuss with people in his office or while on the phone.

Not once did he share with me or anyone else in the meetings or on the shop floor about the need, application, or use of that reference document. He would only say, regarding a bus issue, "It's in Title 13." I would often think, *What the hell is Title 13, and why is it so important?* The director was interesting in his own right, and I suspect it was an intentional choice on his part not to share the information. He seemingly embraced and appeared to enjoy the exclusive right and power of information contained between the book covers.

Interestingly, when we traveled to Lamar, Colorado, to visit the Neoplan bus manufacturing plant there, it was again under his arm. I finally learned the book was *Title 13 California Code of Regulation*, with which the manufacturer was required, by law, to comply for the bus build. Unfortunately for many of us, he didn't share the compliance information within the document and the role it played during the manufacture of the buses, and until his retirement I never saw him share or discuss the significance of the document. It was likely a very selfish, intentional act to covet the information for himself. Let us resist the temptation not to share information; instead, provide it freely!

My closing and sincere remarks regarding this story are that regulatory compliance information, legal resource documents, and the Motor Carrier inspection process must be shared by all, especially with whoever is responsible for audits, accident investigations, new bus procurements, and/or numerous other activities that may involve law enforcement, the CHP, or any other transit-related entity that will apply the language of the law. Knowledge is exciting and at times tempting to covet. Therefore, I urge you to embolden others with the power of information and knowledge and give it away with reckless abandon. It just may save somebody's job!

> *Be advised: A vague or weak understanding of commercial vehicle law may directly affect the overall safety, performance, and inspection readiness of your fleet. Regulatory compliance is essential... it's the law!*

Here are the answers to the questions that were asked on pages 20–21.

1. A *short standing* vehicle defect could have occurred upon pull-in, prior to the Terminal inspection. Example: A tire sidewall might be cut to the cord, which may have occurred when hitting a curb outside the division at pull-in. Upon inspection by the MCS, the vehicle will be removed from service for tire damage. However, since it could have possibly just occurred, it is considered a short standing defect and will not go against the overall Rating of the Terminal. If you're going to experience a Hold bus, you want a short standing defect.

    A *long standing* vehicle defect should have been found and repaired prior to an inspector's finding it. Example: A brake chamber hose is chaffed to the cord. It did not just occur, rather it took time to wear to a Hold status and should have been previously found and repaired. The vehicle will be removed from service. It is considered a "hard hold" and will go against the overall Rating of the Terminal.

2. 49 CFR is *Title 49 of the Code of Federal Regulations* and is the reference document primarily used for interstate operators, specifically, any commercial vehicle that crosses state lines.

    13 CCR is *Title 13 of the California Code of Regulation* for commercial vehicle operators within the state of California. It's an important reference document used by the CHP/Motor

Carrier Specialists and other vehicle compliance authorities.

3. *Title 13 California Code of Regulation* §1212.

4. Yes, 13 CCR adopts CVSA. CVSA is the *Commercial Vehicle Safety Alliance Out-of-Service Criteria Handbook*, which determines if a commercial vehicle is considered Out-of-Service based on maximum allowable limits for vehicle component defects, condition, steering free play, driver requirements, air and/or fuel loss, brake system defects, and other related violations covered in this guide.

5. Primarily in the *Commercial Vehicle Safety Alliance Out-of-Service Criteria Handbook.*

6. After 12 hours of on-duty time, a logbook is required of the bus driver.

7. This is Verification of Transit Training, and it refers to the no-less-than-8-hours' training required each year from birthday to birthday. It is found in the Education Code §40085.5 at the back of the *California Vehicle Code.*

8. A Pull-Notice is also known as the Driver License Monitoring System. It monitors drivers who possess a commercial driver license. It displays their current public driver record as recorded by the California Department of Motor Vehicles. An agency is subject to an annual Pull-Notice inspection and is issued a performance Rating as cited in CVC §1808.1.

9. Secondary employment, either drive or non-drive time, requires the bus driver to file a log (grid graph).

10. Drivers are in violation if they drive after accumulating 80 hours on-duty in any 8 consecutive days.

4

Compliance:
Matters Regulated

Authority cited: California Vehicle Code, *§34501 (a) (1)*
Matters Regulated

The Cambridge dictionary defines the word *compliance* as "The act of obeying an order, rule or request." As a public transit operator, you have an obligation and the awesome responsibility to ensure that your bus and non-revenue fleet are safe, reliable, and compliant, as required by state and federal law, regulations, codes, and the Commercial Vehicle Safety Alliance. Further, as a public transit operator, you are required to obey the law, comply with commercial vehicle safety regulations, and ensure that the equipment is properly maintained, that drivers comply with general driving requirements, and that all Matters Regulated are followed.

The *California Vehicle Code* (CVC), §34501 (a) (1), states that the Department of the California Highway Patrol (Department) has the authority, enacted by the California state legislature, to adopt rules and regulations for commercial vehicles and to ensure full compliance with the law through safety inspections more commonly referred to in the industry as the Annual Safety Compliance Inspection, for all commercial vehicles, including buses. The Basic Inspection of Terminal, Pull-Notice Program, or Employer Notification Program and Drug and Alcohol inspections are also required.

> *Note: The Biennial Inspection of Terminal program and program name has been changed effective January 2016. BIT vehicles are still required to be inspected on a 90-day interval; however, a BIT inspection by the CHP is no longer required every 2 years, and the program name has changed from Biennial Inspection of Terminal to Basic Inspection of Terminal. Contact your Motor Carrier Specialist I, II, or III for the details.*

The Triennial Performance Review/Audit is conducted by an independent third-party inspector once every 3 years and is not audited by the CHP. Rather, it's a performance review for some transit agencies in California that are funded through the Regional Transportation Planning Agency. The audit is required of the Federal Transit Administrator (FTA) to determine if a grantee is following FTA rules and policy. The Triennial Audit is announced in advance, and the inspection criteria and process are discussed in a scheduled preaudit meeting. The audit is a thorough review of process and procedures, as required, within numerous departments, to assess the performance of the operator.

The Department's Motor Carrier Specialists will inspect your Terminal(s) at least once every 13 months, according to CVC §34501 (c), from a representative vehicle sample.

The inspection will include but is not limited to vehicle condition, the maintenance program, driver records, driver Hours-of-Service and service logs (grid graph), if required, and any Out-of-Service vehicle conditions that are identified. Both the Maintenance and Transportation departments will be inspected, generally within 1 day, while the Pull-Notice and Drug and Alcohol inspections may occur at the same time or be scheduled at a later date, based on varying factors.

After the CHP has concluded its inspection, the Terminal is Rated. Only one compliance Rate is issued, and it reflects the true and accurate overall condition of the Terminal against the laws and regulations at the time of inspection. (See Figure 1 in Chapter 6.) The compliance Rating will either be Satisfactory, Unsatis-factory, or Conditional. (The definitions are cited in the *California Code of Regulation Title 13*, §1233.) If the Terminal is Rated Unsatisfactory, it will be re-inspected within 120 days after the issuance of the Rating. Upon re-inspection, if adequate improvement is found, a Conditional Rating will most likely be issued. And while we're on the Terminal Rating issue, let me dispel the commonly perceived notion that Terminals are or can be Rated pass or fail. The authority cited in the

Vehicle Code is clear and unwavering: Terminals and administrative inspections are never Rated pass or fail, but rather Satisfactory, Unsatisfactory, or Conditional.

Again, many transit professionals have not been properly trained in commercial vehicle law and therefore do not understand how the MCS inspectors arrive at a Rating decision. Thus they struggle to find the reference documents that dictate how the inspectors determine the efficiency and effectiveness of a Maintenance and Transportation program. Further, having only a vague understanding of commercial vehicle law and not fully understanding the importance of maintaining a safe and compliant agency is really not an option; it's the law, and it must be understood and managed by staff specifically within the Maintenance and Transportation departments. The Drug and Alcohol and Federal Triennial audits are generally a team effort supported by Maintenance, Transportation, Human Resources and administration personnel.

For the California public transit operator, much is required of many to include having a good understanding of regulatory compliance. Buses must be properly maintained and serviced regularly against a well-defined maintenance plan, records must reflect the true and accurate condition of the equipment, and drivers must comply with Hours-of-Service regulations to include Transit Training, Proficiency, logbook documentation, and other compliance requirements, discussed in later chapters, must be met.

Unfortunately, when individuals at nearly all levels within an agency are questioned on or about a compliance rule or Out-of-Service driver or vehicle condition, they often, and without critical knowledge of the different regulations, state they can be found in the Federal Code. Upon further questioning it quickly becomes apparent the individual(s) possesses minimal knowledge, if any, of the rules and regulations that apply to commercial vehicle operators. Unfortunately, it's the all-too-common charade some play when it's easier to respond with an inappropriate answer than to appear ignorant.

Let me be perfectly clear. In the world of transit regulations and when you're in a position to quickly respond without hesitation, there is no excuse for guessing regarding the law, especially when at a crash event or incident scene or in a court of law. Too often people with limited or no knowledge of the applicable rules and regulations hurry to provide compliance and regulatory information which, unfortunately, is usually inaccurate.

I begin the Regulatory Compliance training programs with the statement, "Know what you don't know" for a specific reason. It is extremely important to realize in a deep and profound way that a clear and accurate understanding of commercial vehicle law is required of the mechanic in the pit, the driver, and all levels within management who are involved in the compliance effort. They must be familiar with all Matters Regulated that affect their involvement within the organization. Often silence is a person's best friend before citing a regulation, code, or Out-of-Service requirement. It's best to say

"I don't know" and then consult an in-house expert or the CHP Motor Carrier Specialist for the answer.

It is inevitable that someone within your company, at one time or another, will work with an outside agency like the California Highway Patrol or a regulatory entity or will be involved in some discovery for litigation. And one thing is certain: Sooner or later, a bus will be involved in a crash, incident, or unusual event and someone, most likely someone within the agency, will provide either administrative/technical information or service records about the condition of the bus and its history, driver record, and/or other information regarding the incident. Depending on the records or data requested, which may also include company policy, "the most knowledgeable person" assigned must be familiar with some elements of commercial vehicle law and well versed in company policy and should be an individual who is willing and capable to represent the interests of the agency. For these and other reasons, it is critical that every transit develop a person(s) who is properly trained to respond to emergency situations and is conversant in regulatory compliance and policy and understands the agency's mission.

Below is a list of inspection requirements, reference documents and miscellaneous items that the most knowledgeable person(s) must know. Further, they should be familiar with both Maintenance and Transportation department functions, policy, and bus and BIT vehicle compliance, and they should know where to access related information.

Note: Any information, hard copy or electronic, regarding the condition of equipment or driver status or any related information or data submitted to outside agencies such as city officials, regulatory agencies, or other entities, must not be released without the express authorization of appropriate senior staff and county or other council within the company. Moreover, verbal discussions with outside authorities regarding respective events is not recommended without proper authorization.

As such, Annual and BIT inspection requirements, Matters Regulated and other Rated inspections by regulatory entities require a thorough understanding of the required inspections, reference documents, and action items as noted.

Required Inspections:

- Pull-Notice Program
- Drug and Alcohol Program
- Proficiency list
- Annual Safety Compliance Terminal Inspection
- Basic Inspection of Terminal
- Pre-Trip inspection
- Records retention (see Appendix C)
- General Driver Requirements/ Hours-of-Service regulations
- Verification of Transit Training
- CDL/medical certificate file
- Secondary employment list

Reference Documents:

- *California Vehicle Code*
- *Title 13 California Code of Regulation*
- *Commercial Vehicle Safety Alliance Out-of-Service Criteria*
- *Title 49 Code of Federal Regulations* (varying parts)
- *National Fire Protection Association, Codes 10 and 52*

Miscellaneous Requirements and Recommendations:

- Work effectively with the Motor Carrier Specialists
- Become familiar with the Compliance Terminal Inspection process
- Understand the role of a Multidisciplinary Accident Investigation Team (MAIT)
- Understand the purpose and procedure of a Triennial Audit

A compliant program does not just happen. It requires proper training, participation, and advocacy by senior staff. And it must be purposefully developed, planned, and managed so that it continues to be consistently effective. A developing compliance program will also require continued senior-level involvement to ensure the program does not stall; until it becomes institutional, it will require continued oversight by selected individuals throughout the organization, managed by an assigned Compliance Coordinator who has a direct path to upper management.

For the contract service provider, full compliance of the law is not simply a good thing that should occur; rather, it is contractual in many instances. Most contracts for contract service providers have within the "terms and conditions" liquidated damages that typically hold them financially liable if service is compromised, a Terminal is Rated Unsatisfactory, or Matters Regulated are not compliant. Costly liquidated damages can and most likely will be imposed for related violations.

The results of a solid compliance effort founded on good communication and well-developed programs will provide management and others with information to assess the on-going activities, efficiencies, and effective-ness of the major departments within the organization. The results of performance audits and favorable Ratings will be founded on a solid understanding of regulatory compliance, as well as management's inclusion in ensuring quality programs through the direct benefit of training, participation, and team involvement.

5

Reference Documents

Throughout the book I use words and terms regarding the law from regulations, codes, and the *Commercial Vehicle Safety Alliance*, almost as though they are interchangeable, written with the same pen, used similarly throughout the commercial vehicle world and seemingly coming from a single source document. The most experienced commercial vehicle enforcement inspectors and compliance officials use the same terms loosely by intent, because the terms are not as important as the intent of the law, while the "basic" spoken word conveys the information more aptly than the legal reference.

I share this with you because I want to convey how very easy it is to get mired in a "Who's on first?" scenario with commercial vehicle regulatory language. And as you continue to read, I urge you not to become frustrated with the language as cited in the reference documents, as they will sometimes appear contradictory and not easy to find in the index sections. In this book, you'll be reading from, and ultimately using throughout your transit career, five essential reference documents.

Prior to starting with law versus regulations and the reference documents, a few common misconceptions need to be cleared up regarding compliance terms, and meanings you need to understand, before we begin the process of connecting the regulatory dots:

- The Annual Terminal inspection is not annual. Rather, it's a 13-month requirement, as cited in CVC §34501 (c).

- Terminal Ratings, Pull-Notice, BIT, and administrative audits are never Rated "pass" or "fail." Rather, they are Rated Satisfactory, Unsatisfactory, or Conditional.

- Many tend to think that the only transit regulation that applies is the Federal Code. Let me explain. The Federal Code that many attempt to reference is *49 Code of Federal Regulations* (Transportation) which is dis-cussed in this chapter. However, the code is primarily applicable for interstate commercial vehicle operators like the "over the road folks." California transits (intrastate operators) pri-marily reference *Title 13, California Code of Regulation* for compliance/enforcement because their operation base resides within the state of California. Because of the Supremacy Clause, Article VI, Section 2, of the U.S. Constitution, all state laws are recognized if they meet or exceed the language of the federal law.

- The Verification of Transit Training requirement of 8 hours per year is not required annually by calendar year; rather, it is based on the driver's birth date.

- BIT now stands for Basic Inspection of Terminal and applies to trucks.

- Adverse driving conditions cited in *California Code of Regulation* §1201 (a) are often referred to simply as "acts of God." And a long train is not considered an adverse driving condition.

- There are no reference documents titled Department of Transportation (DOT). Instead, the laws and regulations governing the California intrastate commercial vehicle operator are referenced in the five primary documents discussed in this book.

- None of the laws, regulations, codes, or alliance information carries any more authority in a court of law than another. A violation of any compliance issue from either resource document referenced in the book is simply a regulatory violation.

Further, the words *law, code, alliance,* and *regulations* will probably always be used interchangeably because, well, there is no absolute science to the use of regulatory compliance words and terms. Become familiar with the documents, learn the general meaning of the words and phrases, and you'll be able to communicate like an authority with Motor Carrier Specialists, commercial enforcement personnel, legal entities, and others.

The book explains the difference between the uses of the words primarily for technical reasons so you will thoroughly understand their differences. Rather than being terminology specific every time, it's much more important to know in what reference document the answers to the questions can be found or what the requirements of the law are, by document and section.

Laws, regulations, codes, and Alliance regulations carry the same weight as law within a court of law and the legal system; but their authority comes from different resource documents and often multiple documents when a reference is adopted from another source.

Statutory Law

Laws are statutes enacted by the United States congress or the state legislature. They are more accurately referred to as *statutory law*, whereby the elected officials (state legislature) approve or disapprove, change the language, or amend the document in any way, whether the law is enacted or not. Specifically I am referring to the *California Vehicle Code*. The Code is not commercial-vehicle specific and covers a wide array of information for most all types of motorized vehicles, registration information, licensing, accident and accident reporting, and offenses, violations, and penalties, to name a few.

Regulations

Regulations are rules adopted by federal and state agencies. The purpose of regulations is to give detail to laws that are expressed in general language and are designed to be more readily (easily) changed than statutory law.

The Office of Administrative Law (OAL) ensures that agency regulations are clear, necessary, legally valid, and available to the public. And every regulation is subject to the rule-making process of the Administrative Procedure Act unless exempted by statute. Again, the intent of the process is to make the regulations more easily amended than those of the *California Vehicle Code, which* requires state legislative action.

The OAL is responsible for reviewing regulations proposed by many state agencies for compliance with the standards set forth in the California Administrative Procedure Act (CAPA). CAPA transmits the regulations to the Secretary of State for publishing in the *California Code of Regulation*, of which there are 28 different titles. And since the book was written exclusively for the California public transit operator, it primarily focuses on *Title 13, California Code of Regulation*, as well as other related documents listed later in this chapter.

Many years ago, one of my college Spanish instructors fluent in nine languages told us at the beginning of the class, "The key to learning a foreign language is to first learn the skeleton of the language and verb conjugation." I've never forgotten those words. Like learning a new language, so it is with learning the language, content, and intent of commercial vehicle law. It starts with the skeleton or basis for knowing what the law says and how to apply it. In the case of regulatory compliance, it is imperative to know where to find the information by reference and section, determine how it will be blended into your fleet/agency programs, and then incorporate the compliance action as necessary. The required information necessary for all transits to follow is found in the six separate and distinct reference documents listed in the next section.

Required Reference Documents

- *Commercial Vehicle Safety Alliance North American Standard Out-of-Service Criteria* (CVSA)

- *Title 13, California Code of Regulation* (13 CCR)

- *Title 49, Code of Federal Regulations* (varying parts)

- *California Vehicle Code*

- *National Fire Protection Association, Codes 10 and 52* (NFPA; two separate documents applicable to public transit operators)

See Appendix B for images of the covers of each of these documents.

Commercial Vehicle Safety Alliance North American Standard Out-of-Service Criteria. According to the *Commercial Vehicle Safety Alliance North American Standard Out-of-Service Criteria Handbook*:

> The CVSA is an international non-profit organization comprised of local, state, provincial, territorial and federal motor carrier safety officials and industry representatives from the United States, Canada and Mexico.

The Commercial Vehicle Safety Alliance is one of the preeminent reference documents that provides regulatory information, Out-of-Service criteria for commercial vehicles and buses for licensing, driver record of duty status, critical vehicle inspection language, inspection levels by the CHP to include most of the Out-of-Service criteria that govern your fleet, and non-revenue (BIT) vehicles and other Matters Regulated. The CVSA is adopted by other reference documents, which include Title 13, CVC, and NFPA, and it is absolutely critical in understanding vehicle Out-of-Service criteria limits (maximum allowable requirements). And though many of the requirements within the CVSA are for "over the road" and other non-bus equipment, much of the information applies to the public transit operator and must be readily available to staff.

The reference documents often adopt each other and will cite other authorities. And since the CVSA applies to both interstate and intrastate, it references the Federal Code and 13 CCR. The information referenced in the *Code of Federal Regulations* for the transits will be cited from Title 49 CFR, Transportation. The

CHP, Motor Carrier Specialists, law enforcement, and other California entities will typically refer to and cite Title 13 for vehicle inspection, crash investigations, and litigation for bus/transit-related matters.

Regulatory compliance documents for public transit operators are as essential to them as repair manuals are to a mechanic. The reference documents should be readily available to mechanics, drivers, supervisors, and managers. Senior management must encourage staff to become familiar with those documents, follow the language of the law, and ensure that departmental programs comply with the regulations specifically covered in the Maintenance Plan and that general driver requirements are followed. The Motor Carrier Specialist only inspects against the language of the laws and regulations and for Out-of-Service violations from the CVSA. Transit personnel/supervisors must resist interpreting the law.

A thorough understanding of laws and regulations that govern a commercial vehicle motor carrier requires the use of the six documents for review, interpretation, and reference for the standard of general information/ application. And it is necessary to say that without the documents, the process of connecting the regulatory dots is nearly impossible without proper training since they each, in various sections, adopt the other documents' language of the law and are found in varying informational detail, depending on the reference.

Let me explain what I just said. The requirements of the law are ultimately the same, whether federal or state; but the depth of information may differ (though the intent remains the same), depending on the specific document referenced. In the case of *Title 49 Code of Federal Regulations*, it primarily addresses the interstate (across state lines) laws for operators that are often different than those of intrastate California transit bus operators and that are found in different Parts of 49 CFR. The federal code is also the likely document for regulations that address drug and alcohol and assessable service, since every state is required to comply with the federal law.

Title 13, California Code of Regulation. Since 1990, Barclays (*www.barclaysccr.com/store*) has been the official publisher of the CCR.

"California Legislature has delegated authority to more than 200 state agencies, boards and commissions to create regulations implementing the State's statutes. All new or amended regulatory language must pass through the California Office of Administrative Law (OAL) for approval. Once completed these laws are filed with the Secretary of State's Office to become enforceable law known as the *California Code of Regulation* (CCR)."

Title 13 of the California Code of Regulation (Title 13) is one of the primary reference documents used by enforcement officers and intrastate operators, and it is often referenced by CHP Motor Carrier Specialists when performing annual Terminal inspections. It's commonly used for providing compliance and other related information for commercial vehicles, California Driver License (CDL) holders, and over-the-road operators, as it references the many regulations pertaining to safe vehicle operations, maintenance, and driver requirements. Like the other reference documents, Title 13 carries the same weight of law through the state legislature, even though it is authorized through the Office of Administrative Law (OAL).

Within the Title 13 document, public transit staff/ personnel can find vital commercial-vehicle–related information. The following issues are frequently brought up, and the references can be found in noted sections of Title 13:

- §615.1 Inspection and Maintenance Stations
- §1087 Tire Condition and Use (also found in CVSA)
- §1213 (d) Driver Record of Duty Status (secondary employment)
- §1214 Driver Fatigue
- §1215 Vehicle Condition (pre-trip)
- §1217 Transportation of Passengers (in step-well area and standing)
- §1230 Damaged Vehicle (drive from location by a qualified person)
- §1234 Required Records for Motor Carriers (records retention)
- §1242 Fire Extinguisher Requirement (note §1242 (c) Exception)
- §1267 Bus Entrances and Exits (note (iii) indicates that buses with a 4-inch or larger gap between the power doors shall be checked with a 1-inch-diameter smooth cylinder)

- §1269.1 Equipment for Transporting Wheelchairs
- §1270 (a) Bus Driver Seat

Title 49, Code of Federal Regulations. "49 CFR is the codification of the general and permanent rules published in the Federal Register by the Executive Department and agencies of the Federal Government."

For California public transit operators, 49 CFR is a reference document for Matters Regulated, regarding federal law requirements, to include Drug and Alcohol and the Americans with Disabilities Act laws. It is also the recommended source document for interstate commerce, since those operators regularly cross state lines. California public transit operators should refer mainly to 13 CCR for regulatory guidance.

49 CFR consists of different "Parts," and for the public transit operator they should refer to the recommended documents: 49 CFR Parts 300–399 for the Federal Motor Carrier Safety Regulations, Part 382 for Drug and Alcohol, and Parts 400–599 for the Federal Motor Vehicle Safety Standards.

California Vehicle Code. The Code is an excellent resource document for most everything that has from small to large wheels, including the big-rig combinations that operate throughout California's roadways. Numerous commercial vehicle compliance issues, including bus equipment, driver requirements, stopping distance, and much more information, are available in the code. And take my advice, become familiar with how to use the index section to ultimately find answers to your questions, if not provided in this book, or contact your local Motor Carrier Specialist unit for assistance.

If I had a nickel for every time I called the Southern Division of the CHP throughout the years, I'd be Rockefeller. However, before calling, conduct your due diligence and make an attempt to locate the information on your own. It will help you become more familiar with the regulations and will demonstrate to the authorities that you and the agency are serious about understanding and applying commercial vehicle law.

All of the reference documents will require time and some patience for familiarization. The information from within the documents may be new to you and will require a reasonable amount of time for you to become efficient in finding the information required, especially when you're referred to other documents (adopted documents). The Vehicle Code is no different; it will regularly refer you to Title 13, CVSA, 49 CFR, or the NFPA codes.

The Vehicle Code is readily available at most all Department of Motor Vehicles offices and costs about ten dollars.

National Fire Protection Association® Codes 10 and 52. (The NFPA is an International Codes and Standards Organization.) NFPA is widely recognized and provides many products and services; training on fire, electrical and building safety; and much more. However, public transit operators and contract service providers need only subscribe to *NFPA 10, Standard for*

Portable Fire Extinguishers, and *NFPA 52, Vehicular Gaseous Fuel Systems Code.*

For the transits, and for purpose of this book relative to bus operations, NFPA 10 applies to the selection, inspection, maintenance, and testing of portable fire extinguishers on buses. The document covers general responsibility, persons performing the maintenance and recharging of extinguishers, required certifications, records maintenance, inspection interval, and much more. Additional information regarding extinguishers for buses is cited in 13 CCR §1242 Fire Extinguishers.

> *Note "exceptions to the extinguisher rule" are cited in 13 CCR §1242 (c).*

Any and all vehicular gaseous fuel issues can be found in NFPA 52.

California Commercial Driver Handbook. This handbook, which is available at most DMV offices, is not a legal reference document, nor is it statutory law, a state/federal regulation, or an Out-of-Service guide. It is, however, a valuable source of information for the commercial vehicle operator, specifically regarding the CDL rules that apply to operators of bus, BIT vehicles, and other regulated equipment. It references state and federal authority for vehicle inspection, vehicle control, transporting of passengers, air brake systems, pre-trip requirements, and much more. It is a recommended reference document to be kept at the Maintenance and Transportation departments.

A good understanding of commercial vehicle law requires training, document ownership, and a commitment to understand the application of the compliance language for your bus and non-revenue fleet, driver requirements, and others involved in vehicle inspection and general compliance readiness activities.

Note that commercial vehicle rules and regulations are not found in any "one" of the listed documents. And there is no single reference document or source that will direct you to the law or a section exclusive to the public transit operator. Within the six documents are the regulations for tankers, combination vehicles, public transit buses, school buses, school pupil activity buses, general public para-transit vehicles, and other regulated commercial vehicles. The defining list of what is considered a regulated vehicle is easily found in the *California Vehicle Code* §34500.

As you read the book, the regulatory "haze" will begin to disappear and you will experience a greater understanding of how the regulations and compliance process work together in a reasonable semblance of order. Just trust me.

One of the reference documents, for example, the Out-of-Service criteria for "maximum allowables" under CVSA does not reflect general/conventional regulatory language. Rather it is the primary document used to reference if a commercial vehicle is potentially unsafe for service. A maximum allowable is the maximum length, travel, air loss, free play, crack length, or any other condition that suggests a vehicle is unsafe to operate and could possibly cause an accident or a crash, or a vehicle breakdown. The CVSA is an excellent reference document to determine if a bus or non-revenue vehicle is unsafe to operate on the road. However, the CVSA does not cite every maximum allowable requirement for every safety issue regarding a transit bus. And, as you read the document, it will become immediately apparent that much of it was written for "over the road" commercial vehicles. Regardless, the Motor Carrier Inspectors refer to the CVSA for citing Out-of-Service conditions for the Terminal and BIT inspections.

Simply put, a particular section in any of the documents will often refer you to another document for continued information or a more thorough explanation of that part of the law.

For example, in 13 CCR regarding natural gas fueled systems, the document has adopted the National Fire Protection Association Code 52 for you to reference for the definitive language on vehicular fuel system regulation. Often, the state regulation and the CVSA direct you to *Title 49 of the Code of Federal Regulations.* As you become more familiar with the adoption of language to different documents, the process will begin to make sense.

The regulations discussed are readily available for purchase, and the procurement sources for the hard copies can be found in Appendix D of the book. The documents are also available electronically; however, I strongly discourage their exclusive use when looking for a preferred section or performing commercial vehicle law research. Often compliance research or the basic study of the regulations will require an individual to reference multiple documents simultaneously and refer to different sections and documents, all of which I have found to be challenging in the electronic versions when the hard copy serves as a very good medium. Call me old school if you want, but you simply can't highlight or dog-ear electronic versions.

Indeed, it's beneficial and often necessary to highlight, tab and dog-ear various pages and sections in the print version for quick and easy reference. I also recommend ownership of two copies of at least Title 13 and the *California Vehicle Code*, because they will be referenced often. One copy I refer to as the "control document," which should be maintained reasonably clean and updated at all times; the other I refer to as the "working document," which should be accessed for personal use and ends up marked, written upon, highlighted, and generally just abused.

Reference documents are the life blood of a compliance-based organization such as a public transit agency. The documents must command the programs, give direction to regulated activities, hold staff accountable to Matters Regulated, and dictate action such as maintenance practices, driver requirements, record keeping, and all things required by law.

6

The Annual Terminal Inspection

Authority cited: California Vehicle Code *§34501*

Whether you're a transit agency with 50 or 2,050 buses your fleet, maintenance and transportation records, equipment condition, training and other programs will be inspected by the Department of the California Highway Patrol, pursuant to the *California Vehicle Code, Title 13 of the California Code of Regulation*, and the *Commercial Vehicle Safety Alliance*. The inspections are required by law, and the Terminals will be Rated either Satisfactory, Unsatisfactory, or Conditional, as cited in Title 13 CCR §1233.

Further, Terminal inspections are either announced or unannounced, depending on the fleet size. According to CVC §34501 (c), a Terminal inspection for a transit bus operation with more than 100 buses shall be unannounced. Obviously then, any bus operation with a fleet size less than 100 will most always be announced. I do extend a word of caution, however: A year passes quickly, and before you know it, it's that time again and you may find yourself asking whether you're prepared. Division Managers are extremely busy, and time can and will get away from even the most conscientious person. And it may be too late to hope or assume the fleet and related programs are prepared. Previous Satisfactory Ratings are a poor indicator of the condition of the current equipment, driver requirements, or records.

Each quarter, Maintenance and Transportation managers should meet with related staff for a compliance review. The agenda should include status of the preventative maintenance program, required Verification of Transit Training (VTT), Hours-of-Service and log-book status (if required), and an update on any and all maintenance campaign work and records. And with announced inspections, managers and staff should continue to meet quarterly; never relax regarding inspection preparedness!

Continue with all scheduled preventive maintenance, keep your programs current, maintain impeccable records, and expect all shift supervisors to understand and accept the continuing compliance effort. It's been said by too many managers and supervisors, after audits, "Well, that's over, and we won't see them again for a year." Keep CHP alive and well in the hearts and minds of all staff, especially the drivers and mechanics who play such an important role in safety and compliance.

Fleet campaigns are recommended, especially for the larger transits, to help ensure that simple Out-of-Service conditions on bus systems do not magically begin. The campaigns are easily managed and generally quick to perform. They ensure bus safety and preparedness and are well received, even encouraged, by the Motor Carrier Specialists. Typical safety-related campaigns may include brake lights, turn signals, interior-engine-compartment access door integrity, seat and stanchion securement and tire tread depth and sidewall damage inspection. Inside tire damage and airline-to-brake-chamber fouled hoses are occasionally and easily overlooked. These items are Out-of-Service conditions based on the CVSA and will render the bus unsafe for service. When found, they must be immediately repaired before the bus can enter service.

When the CHP safety inspection person or team arrives, and if campaigns are being conducted or have recently occurred, it is wise to present the inspectors with the campaign list(s), as it demonstrates that the agency is taking proactive steps to ensure safe and reliable equipment through in-house, independent campaign programs, while not relying exclusively on mileage-driven preventive maintenance. If the inspectors begin to notice simple defects, they may begin to look more closely at safety-related items when/if they begin to notice redundant and especially minor mechanical trends or driver deficiencies. The overall condition of your equipment, driver and maintenance records, training, and other Matters Regulated immediately expose a perception of the overall condition of the agency's programs and compliance readiness.

A bus, regardless of age, that is reasonably clean, has an uncontaminated chassis, emits no audible air leaks, and draws minimal attention to minor details often will impress the inspector. As I mention throughout the book, the inspectors are observant, technically knowledge-able, fair minded, and very familiar with commercial vehicle regulations. After inspecting two or three buses, they seem to develop an opinion of the condition of the remaining buses that were previously selected. I have also observed that the condition of the first few buses, in both cleanliness and equipment, assuredly will set the tone and pace of the audit. On the Transportation side, ensure that the CDL and medical certificates are current, the Pull-Notice is reviewed often, Transit Training (8-hour requirement) is compliant, and logbooks are complete, dated, and signed. All of this is covered in Chapter 8.

The safety compliance Rating issued by the Motor Carrier Inspector(s) reflects the Terminal's overall com-pliance against applicable law and regulations that govern the maintenance program, number of Out-of-Service buses, driver Hours-of-Service requirement, transit training hours, and driver requirements. The Terminal will receive one Rating for both the Mainte-nance and Transportation departments. Therefore it is incumbent for both to be compliant with all Matters Regulated, because the "single" Rating affects everyone. See Figure 1.

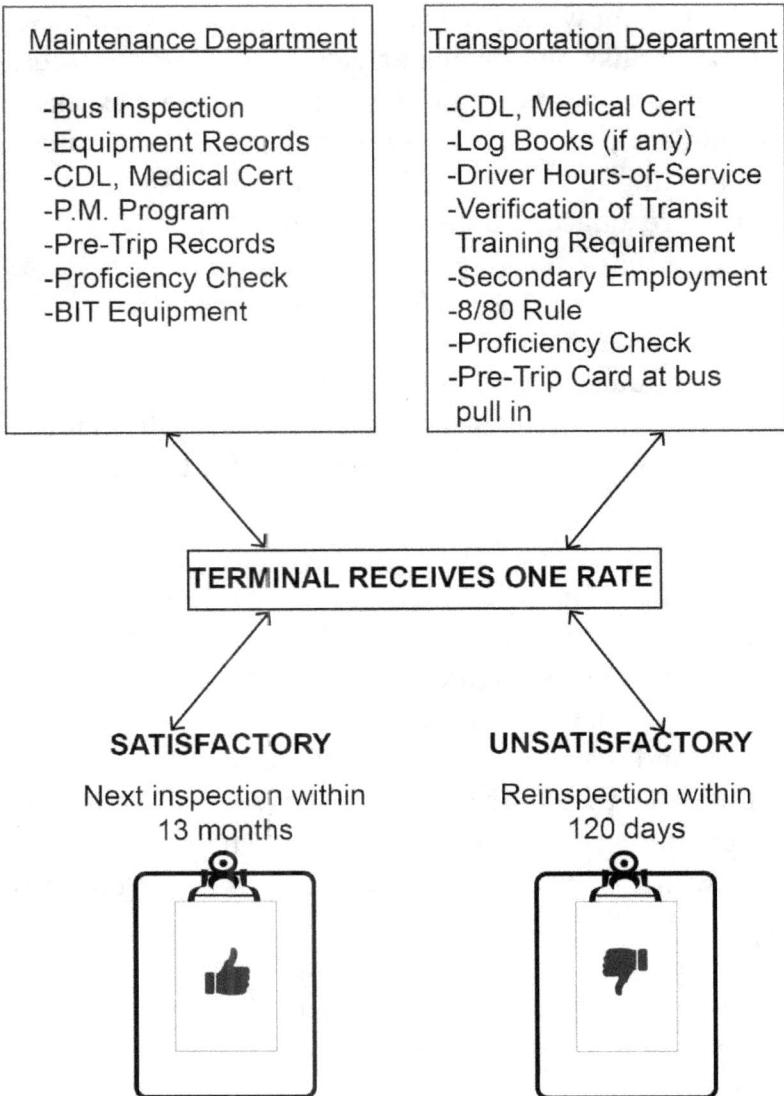

Figure 1. California Highway Patrol Terminal Compliance Audit.

I have known agencies to receive an Unsatisfactory Rating exclusively for bus drivers exceeding the Hours-of-Service regulations, not filing logbooks, for excessive Out-of-Service equipment requirement violations, and/or for missing or improperly managed records, all of which are unacceptable. The annual Terminal inspection generally occurs close to the same month of the last inspection. Therefore, it's recommended that a few months prior to inspection (regardless of the recommended quarterly meeting), both the Maintenance and Transportation managers, unless it's a single-manager concept, begin their strategy meetings for the upcoming Terminal inspection.

Some of you are already thinking that your programs are adequate and always ready for the scrutiny of an audit. And I say that's wonderful and cautiously admirable. But some staff members transfer in and out of different divisions and others occasionally retire or resign, and new and less experienced people are placed in positions they may be unfamiliar with, which is often the compliance side of the business. The fact is, not all staff want to be involved in the regulatory effort or involved with the Terminal inspection process. And it isn't like that's all they have to do, right? Welcome to the world of regulatory compliance, commercial vehicle enforcement, and having to expose your hard work to inspector(s) who will make or ruin your day based on a single Rating.

If you've never experienced an Unsatisfactory Terminal or administrative Rating, congratulations; I'm certain you've worked hard to attain that level of accomplishment. But let me assure you that if you receive the unenviable Unsatisfactory Rating, it will quickly become a very nasty "who's who in the zoo" type day, regardless of whether it's on Maintenance, Transportation, or a combination of both.

Let's pause for a serious reality check. Consider, just consider, the unpleasant thought of having to inform your department head, who will then inform the CEO, who will then inform the Board Chair, that his or her agency has just received an Unsatisfactory CHP Terminal Rating for excessive and generally inexcusable violations. From senior and executive management to the Board, a litany of questions will be asked that require detailed/specific answers. Also be prepared to explain how the programs failed and describe your definitive course of action to reverse the situation. Chapter 10 covers recommendations on how to resolve an Unsatisfactory Rating.

And know this: Unsatisfactory Ratings happen more often than you may realize. That's typically because staff become distracted or else overconfident with their programs (pride precedes the fall); or in some instances there is a change in management or staff responsibilities. Further, I am amazed at how many people within the Maintenance and Transportation departments don't know what is required of them or the agency, as related to commercial vehicle law, driver requirements, or the many requirements that govern regulated vehicles. For example, the 10-hour drive rule is often confused with the 12-hour on-duty time requirement; mechanics who road test or "road call" buses sometimes do not pre-trip their vehicle as required; and many supervisors do not have a basic understanding of the Pull-Notice Program or the Proficiency check as required by law.

I raise these issues not to be mean spirited or overly critical of Division Managers, supervisors, and/or transit instructors, but rather to expose some issues now, in this book, before they become *very serious issues later*. Later, meaning while you're at home, relaxing in front of the flat screen watching the news, when a reporter starts with a developing story about one of your buses that was involved in a crash that resulted in multiple injuries and/or fatalities. Granted, it isn't a pleasant thought, but public transit, school bus, and general public para-transit vehicle crashes happen more often than we realize.

My advice? Safety first and regulatory laws and regulations second. Always be in compliance, communication, and knowledge; it's critical of a world-class transit organization. And keep CHP, regulatory inspectors, and enforcement officials close and well informed about your agency.

7

CHP Terminal Inspection: Maintenance Department

Authority Cited: CVC §34501, Matters Regulated

As a commercial vehicle operator, you are required by the Department of the California Highway Patrol to submit to Safety Compliance Terminal inspections, according to CVC §34501 of vehicles referenced in CVC §34500, which include buses and non-bus (BIT) vehicles such as tow trucks, trailers, parts trucks, Facility Maintenance rolling stock, or any other regulated piece of equipment based on length, weight, hazardous material, or commodity transported. Buses are subject to an annual inspection, whereas the non-bus (BIT) equipment is inspected based on California Performance Safety Scores.

Further, as listed in Appendix A, Pillars for Regulatory Compliance by Department, the MCS will evaluate the overall condition of your equipment, the overall maintenance program, its effectiveness, maintenance records, driver Proficiency, Pull-Notice, CDL, medical certificate, and the BIT program. The overall preventative maintenance program should mirror the agency's program as written into the Maintenance Plan, wherein preventative maintenance inspections, typically by mileage, are determined almost exclusively by the agency. The MCS will inspect against your program, the condition of the buses, and records and will list any and all deficiencies, violations, and Out-of-Service conditions. Remember: The Maintenance Department inspection is only one component in the overall Terminal Rating.

Although commonly referred to as the CHP *Annual* Safety Terminal Review, by law the requirement is a 13-month inspection interval, as cited in CVC §34501 (c). Regardless, the CHP, under the authority of the state legislature, is mandated to adopt reasonable rules and regulations to help promote the safe operation of buses and other regulated vehicles. And it is authorized to prohibit the operation of vehicles with violations against the law, meaning it has the legal authority to place buses Out-of-Service until proper repairs are made. Often the agency is authorized to repair Out-of-Service vehicles during an inspection; however, there is no guarantee the inspector will not count the violation as a hard hold against the overall Rate.

You'll find that attitude, respect, cooperation, and assistance sometimes go a long way with an inspector's decision regarding a hold condition versus an equipment requirement violation, which is not a hold condition. The CHP has the authority to authorize an immediate repair or adjustment to prevent holding the equipment, which could be the difference between a Satisfactory or Unsatisfactory Rating, depending on the current number of violations.

As required, the CHP Motor Carrier Specialist(s) will conduct an inspection at your Terminal, evaluate the bus maintenance program, remove buses for Out-of-Service conditions (if necessary), check for valid CDL and medical certificates, and determine proper records management, driver requirements, and other inspection criteria listed in Appendix A.

Shortly after the MCSs arrive, they will either select the buses themselves as they return from "tripper or short run" service, or, in some instances, request agency representatives participating in the inspection to pull the representative sample of buses. Generally they want buses that reflect a reasonable mix of each series type, if possible, assigned to the division. Buses on the Dead List or being held for any number of reasons are not selected as inspection candidates. And if you've never experienced this before, don't be surprised if the MCS asks the dispatcher to relieve a bus or buses from revenue service on an "okay change, no time lost" basis as part of their inspection sample.

Though it has been uncommon, I have personally experienced such requests. For unknown reasons, the Motor Carrier Unit directed staff to have the Dispatcher pull buses without explanation or reason. I was later informed that someone, possibly within the agency, whose name was intentionally left anonymous by the CHP, reported that the agency was allegedly not performing the required preventative maintenance and the buses could be operating unsafe. The few times I experienced buses removed from service off the street for a Terminal inspection, no unsafe conditions were revealed, the buses showed no evidence of improper maintenance, and equipment records were satisfactory.

Regardless, their motives are not personal and the actions are within their authority to remove the equipment from service. And though they can and should be challenged about that type of request, I recommend that you "first comply and then ask why."

As previously mentioned in the book, the inspectors anticipate technical and procedural questions from staff and are always willing to explain their decisions and actions, but they will not tolerate an unruly confrontation or any form of hostility. That type of behavior will further aggravate the situation, especially if profanity is used and/or if defiance is perceived. Overzealous staff at any level, either represented or management, must immediately be removed from the inspection area.

At a Terminal inspection I attended, two MCSs were in a pit inspecting the bus undercarriage for compliance when the First-Shift Supervisor insisted that I tell the inspectors to stop work until they both put on bump caps. Well, as the story goes, they continued inspecting the buses, sans bump caps, and the Supervisor was directed to leave the inspection area until further notice. The division was ultimately rated Satisfactory with minimal equipment requirement violations and no

Out-of-Service defects. And for those of you policy-minded people wondering if the agency/division had a bump cap policy, yes, they did. To that I say it is widely understood that *sometimes* in the interest of *something* beneficial, it's *sometimes* prudent to *sometimes* modify the policy for the agency's best interest in the situation. Let's move on; I'm sure you get my point.

After the buses have been selected for inspection, they are essentially on hold under the authority of the inspector; and other than for parking and staging purposes, they must not be worked on by a mechanic for any purpose unless expressly authorized by the inspector. What I mean by "worked on" is using any tool or device on the bus for purpose of adjusting, repairing, or fixing any component that appears loose or requires tightening. No part(s) shall be removed, replaced, or modified as to render the bus in a different condition other than when it was selected for inspection.

I assure you, the inspectors will not be forgiving if the condition of the bus is compromised. Don't believe me? Get caught and find out for yourself. It may be your first and fastest Out-of-Service bus ever experienced! At a minimum you will most likely be embarrassed and/or cautioned for the activity. And they may request a different bus to inspect. Accordingly it is essential that staff, especially those assigned to work directly with the inspectors, be informed well in advance that related actions must be discussed with and authorized only by the inspector. Often mechanics are uninformed regarding those types of unacceptable activities, which can quickly create a bad situation. For that and other important reasons, the mechanics selected to work with the MCSs must fully understand the inspection process and know the requirements, such as not altering a bus's condition once it has been selected for inspection.

Understand that the annual Terminal inspection event is a tango, not a simple dance, and all components of it should be well choreographed and thoroughly communicated to division personnel, including supervisors, mechanics, and service attendants/cleaners on all shifts. I say that because, and especially for, the new employees, since it may be a new experience to have the CHP at the facility. They eagerly want to know why they're on the property, what they are doing, and how the Terminal is Rated. Daily or weekly safety meetings are a good time to inform staff about the Terminal and/or BIT inspections and the compliance requirements mandated by law. Similarly, new management staff at all levels from the Maintenance and Transportation departments should receive a basic overview of the inspection process and the seriousness of compliance review.

Anyone involved with assisting in the Terminal inspection is responsible to ensure that the basic preparatory needs are met before it begins. Inspectors require and appreciate a safe, well-lit pit or work area, free of trip hazards and debris. Also a stand-up desk in the shop often used by "leaders" or even a tool-box lid works well for them to enter data into the computer as they note deficiencies, violations, or any Out-of-Service condition.

The number of buses selected for the Terminal audit, either by the inspector or the agency, if authorized by the inspector, is commonly known as the "Representative Sample," similar to that in CVC §34501.12. Contrary to what many think, the number of buses to fleet size selected for inspection is not arbitrary but rather formula based. And their intent is to select the required number of buses with a reasonable mix by bus type and vehicle age.

Note the following represented bus fleet sizes and BIT sample sizes:

Fleet Size	Representative Sample of Equipment
1 to 2	All
3 to 8	3
9 to 15	4
16 to 25	6
26 to 50	9
51 to 90	14
91 or more	20

Whether the Terminal inspection is announced or unannounced, or whether it's a small or large-sized agency, inspectors use the same reference documents and inspection protocol, follow similar procedures, and generally apply them consistently against commercial vehicle law. What is not always the same is the inspection process they use to acquire information and data, the amount of time they spend at an agency to complete an audit, and, depending, they may or may not perform the Pull-Notice and/or Drug and Alcohol inspection at that time. At smaller agencies, the MCSs often return for 2 or 3 consecutive days to complete the Terminal audit and may or may not include the Pull-Notice Program and the Drug and Alcohol inspection with the Terminal audit. If they include the administrative Pull-Notice and/or Drug and Alcohol inspections into the annual Terminal inspection, each of the inspections is Rated independently. And again, depending on the fleet size and available inspectors, they may also perform a BIT inspection if required.

At mid to large-size agencies, the Pull-Notice and Drug and Alcohol inspections generally occur months later and are almost always announced.

Unless otherwise notified, the MCSs will follow the Level V inspection format referenced in the CVSA. There are seven different inspection levels, and all are presented in the CVSA, on the inside of the front and rear cover. Level V is the most commonly used inspection for the public transit operator. If the inspection level type changes, your agency will typically be notified by the Motor Carrier Specialist III Unit Supervisor, prior to the inspection.

The seven levels of inspection are as follows:

- Level I: North American Standard Inspection
- Level II: Walk-Around Driver/Vehicle Inspection
- Level III: Driver Credential Inspection
- Level IV: Special Inspections
- Level V: Vehicle-Only Inspection

- Level VI: North American Standard Inspection for Transuranic Waste and Highway Route Controlled Quantities of Radioactive Material
- Level VII: Jurisdictional Mandated Commercial Vehicle Inspection

It is essential that staff who are assigned to work with the inspector(s) during the audit are knowledgeable about the maintenance program, reasonably friendly, and somewhat familiar with commercial vehicle regulations as applied to the equipment, records, and driver requirements. I strongly recommend against making the mistake of some agencies, that when the team arrives, management performs a quick meet and greet (traditionally on the maintenance department shop floor), secures the buses requested by the inspector, and then vanishes until the audit concludes, evaluation Rating is determined, and the document is awaiting signature.

If the Terminal inspection is not supported by the agency, it demonstrates a lack of interest, which is not well received by most inspectors. Further, it spoils a good learning opportunity for mechanics and/or supervisor and will not allow the agency to register a verbal challenge with the inspector should a bus be held Out-of-Service or for any other major violation(s) that may go against the overall Terminal Rating.

Although it's uncommon, an inspector, generally an apprentice MCS, has been known to render a bus or buses Out-of-Service when in fact they may not be. For that reason and others, it's wise for the agency to have present, throughout the entire inspection process, representatives who are familiar with commercial vehicle law and, for Maintenance, understand the "maximum allowable" criteria mentioned within the CVSA Guide. As most of us know, knowledge is power; without it, you're at the mercy of an inspector who might have made an unintentional mistake that could possibly make the difference between a Satisfactory or Unsatisfactory Rating.

Regardless of fleet size, a good rule to follow is to assign one mechanic to each inspector; and for a mid to large-sized fleet, also assign a mechanic to stage/park buses and to secure parts and tools if necessary. The inspectors have only a few tools in their possession that they use to perform their duties. Some have additional tools inside their van; however, it's inconvenient for them to access their vehicle when tools are readily available in the shop and time is limited. Offering tools, assistance, and parts, whenever required, helps to establish a solid working relationship that is built on professional courtesy and respect.

The inspectors are performing their duties, as required, to the best of their ability, and one of their top priorities is to ensure that buses and all other commercial vehicles operating on the roads and highways are safe and properly maintained to prevent crashes and injury. Therefore, help them achieve their mission by being respectful and supportive throughout the inspection, and partner with them during all phases of the process, from "meet and greet" to signatory accepting the overall Rating for the Terminal. A properly maintained fleet with accurate and well-managed records and driver requirements, combined with a respectful atmosphere, will most always result in a favorable Rating.

The truth about audits, reviews, and inspections is that you and your staff may be temporarily inconvenienced, the arrival time of the inspector(s) may interfere with the roll-out and some of your work for 1 or 2 days, and you or someone else must be prepared to explain Maintenance Department processes, procedures, and the equipment maintenance programs to questioning inspectors.

When the CHP Motor Carrier Team, Triennial audit consultants, or any legal authority is on the property, it is important they be treated with the utmost respect and assisted in every way. Similarly, if a bus is involved in a major crash or incident that involves injuries or fatalities, you will very possibly have CHP inspectors, attorneys, legal representatives, and/or others requesting bus maintenance history, driver records, and current equipment information.

They too must always be treated respectfully and assured they will be given full support during the investigation or legal discovery and that assistance is available at any time if requested. Equally important, it's absolutely necessary to inform your staff who assist entities of authority during an investigation, that they should answer questions only to the best of their knowledge and ability, keep the answers brief, and refrain from personal opinion.

Assisting staff must also know that the words "I don't know" are appropriate and, at times, very wise. Guessing (conjecture) is almost never recommended unless the inspector or legal entity expressly asks for a guess. The statements made in discovery or upon an investigation can and often will be used in a court of law and possibly before a jury. *Barron's Law Dictionary,* Third Edition, regarding the word *conjecture,* states, "A witness may only testify as to facts within his knowledge and may not present conjecture to the jury."

Anatomy of a Terminal Inspection

Whether announced or unannounced, the arrival of the CHP Motor Carrier team will become readily apparent with the arrival of one or more full-sized white vans, usually appearing at the Maintenance Department in the early morning.

The team will formally introduce themselves to the agency representative, supervisor, or Division Manager, or they will greet a known acquaintance less formally if there's a well-established relationship. Less formal is good; it's evidence of a well-fostered relationship and one to strive for when working with the CHP Motor Carrier team.

The following actions should immediately occur upon their arrival:

- Ensure that the Maintenance and Transportation managers are immediately informed of their arrival.

- Inform the Director of Maintenance and Transportation that CHP Motor Carrier Specialist(s) are on the property to perform related inspection(s). Remember, Terminal audits can be announced or unannounced, while administrative inspections are almost always announced. Inform senior staff where they are, the number of inspectors, and the type of audit to be conducted.

- Someone within the agency must take the lead role in managing the audit, and all action items and issues must be coordinated through that individual. That person should remain with the inspector(s) up to the completion of the inspection, which will end with a Terminal Rate and signature. There is no legal requirement for who signs the safety compliance report; however, typically the Maintenance or Transportation Manager is obligated. The Terminal Rate should immediately be communicated to senior staff, to include total number and type of violations, number of buses inspected, and any Out-of-Service equipment and/or driver violations. Accordingly, there should be definitive protocol for this responsibility. Whoever is responsible for the task must be capable, at a minimum, of explaining the inspection process and how a Terminal is Rated. An Unsatisfactory Rating will require a more thorough explanation relative to the non-compliance issues, why the Terminal received the Rate, and what laws or regulations were violated. And then the final and most important question will assuredly be asked—and you guessed it—"How did this happen, and who is responsible?"

- Designate the inspection area and ensure it is clean, well lit; free of debris, grease, and oil; and easily accessible.

- Depending on bus sample size, assign a mechanic to each inspector.

- Within 1 hour of the inspectors' arrival, the Maintenance and Transportation Manager and a senior staff member should meet and welcome the inspectors to the agency and inform them not to hesitate to call if they require anything.

- Offer the use of tools, lighting devices, new batteries for their flashlights, gloves, and writing materials such as pen and paper.

- The inspectors are now using computers at the locations to input the data. If possible, ensure that 110-volt power is available.

- Under the umbrella of professional courtesy, it's recommended that the division, without asking the inspectors, provide coffee, bottled water, and a few donuts at the beginning of the inspection. And again, at your discretion, should the inspection continue through lunch hours, provide the lunch of your choice. Participating mechanics and other support staff should be welcome to partake of both offerings. This act of thoughtfulness is not intended to persuade the inspectors, nor should it be construed as an enticement. I have attended lunch offerings while the same divisions were Rated Unsatisfactory at the end of the day. The decision is yours; know that food offerings and/or beverages are never expected by the MCSs, and some may elect not to accept any food or drink.

- If the inspector(s) are new to the facility, spend a few minutes to introduce key staff and discuss the shop layout/restroom locations, emergency exits, and any other points of interest. Offer a quick tour of the shop, administrative offices, and fuel station/wash rack area.

- If you're a mid to larger transit and the tires are on a "mileage" program, inform the tire service contract provider representative to be available throughout the audit. This person can be a tire service worker, supervisor, or more senior person within the tire company. It isn't uncommon for inspectors to find defective and occasionally illegal tires, because of their severe duty cycle, and they are encouraged when related problems are immediately resolved and unsafe tires quickly replaced. Bus tire tread should never be smooth or under the legal requirements of 4/32 inch front or 2/32 inch rear.

- Agencies with a Maintenance Quality Assurance Department should assign a staff member to attend the inspection.

- A word of caution: Some inspectors do not appreciate a crowd of non-participative individuals "milling" around with their arms folded and pontificating about all things not relevant to a regulatory compliance inspection

while smoking and loudly joking about stuff. My
recommendation? Ask them to leave.

After the "meet and greet" and the buses are being
selected, ask the MCS which inspection Level they will
follow so there is no misunderstanding of the inspection format. Then ask the inspector who will be
reviewing equipment records and how far back
they want the agency to pull the information. If your
system is paperless, at least you'll know how far back to
go electronically.

Typically they will look at about three Preventive
Maintenance (PM) inspection cycles; however, they do
not always review the records of the same number of
inspections at all agencies, every time. If they're familiar
with the Terminal/equipment and their good maintenance program, they may only request one or two PM
cycles back. Then again, they could request more
history, based on issues you are unaware of. Factors
might include reported allegations of improper maintenance, buses in service with Out-of-Service conditions,
or "pencil whipping" the records, to name a few.

Be prepared to make scheduled and unscheduled
work order records available for the selected buses.
They hope to find records that reflect the true and
accurate condition of the equipment and types of
repair(s) completed by the mechanics and expect to
read meaningful explanations of repair work performed. The words "no defect found" or "repaired and
returned to service" do not clearly explain the repair
actions taken. The PM and the unscheduled work documents must show date of completed repair or service,

signed by the mechanic and a foreman/supervisor or person of authority to close the work order or repair card. Either manual or electronic, they expect to see well-documented repair information with completion date, appropriate vehicle number, division number, and proper signatures, if hard copies.

If the fleet size is small (I realize "small" is relative), the inspector will complete the equipment inspection phase before inspecting the maintenance records. In the interest of time, the inspector may return to Transportation the following day to complete the Terminal inspection. Mid-size and larger transits often have multiple inspectors, and at approximately halfway into the equipment inspection an inspector will go to the Transportation side for the driver component of the inspection. As with Maintenance, when they go to Transportation they must be accompanied by a representative from the agency during the audit. (The Transportation audit is covered in the next chapter.)

After conveying how far back to pull the records, the inspector will begin the bus-inspection process by first giving the assigned mechanic a couple of procedural instructions using his or her hands regarding the activation of lights, turn signals, brake lights, and backup lights. More specifically, they will give further instructions while they are under the bus. For safety reasons and because it's often difficult to hear verbal commands when inspecting underneath, especially with the motor running, the mechanic is instructed to apply and hold the brakes when one hard "rap" on the chassis is heard. When two hard "raps" are heard, the mechanic is to release the brakes. This coordinated activity is used when the inspector measures the brake-rod travels on all axles and when inspecting brake-related components, brake-shoe travel, and for air leaks. (Brake-rod travels are found in CVSA under Section 1. Brake Systems.)

With the mechanic situated in the driver seat, the inspector will almost always begin first by inspecting the interior of the bus.

However, before I continue, it's important to know that although the inspector will conduct a visual on literally most every safety and major component on the vehicle, Out-of-Service issues will be cited only for things that may present an unsafe condition for the patrons and the driving public. All other violations are noted as a written equipment-violation discrepancy. Equipment write-ups that are not cited Out-of-Service will not render the bus "held" from service.

For example, if the wheelchair ramp (high-floor bus) or a ramp (low-floor bus) is defective and does not deploy, it will not present an unsafe condition to passengers or the driving public, and the bus can operate safely. Wheelchair systems, functionality, and preventative maintenance are not referenced in the CVSA. For information regarding wheelchair lifts and ramp requirements, refer to ADA regulations in the Code of Federal Regulations.

Once inside the bus, the inspector will begin asking the mechanic to provide information—possibly type of bus, series within their fleet, the VIN, and/or other information. The MCS will discuss the inspection plan and how the work will be coordinated. After those issues are understood, the inspector will begin by asking the mechanic to activate controls and switches and have the mechanic provide assistance that generally requires two people, like inspecting door function and testing sensitive edges. The MCS will observe the mechanic manually operate the controls, switches, and driver seat function and positions, and will inspect the driver area for any unsafe conditions or compliance violation. Often the MCS will direct the mechanic to replace, repair, or tighten components as they deem necessary, or may simply write the item as a defect.

If a bus is removed from service, don't assume the inspector will tell you. After each bus has been inspected, it is prudent to ask if there are any OOS (Out-of-Service) issues with the vehicle or any violations that could be resolved while on the pit or hoist. If the bus has been held from service, quickly determine the violation by discussing the matter with the inspector and then personally look at the violation. For those reasons and others, it is necessary to have a current set of reference documents readily available. An OOS result must be taken seriously, even if it's a "short standing defect." Discuss the issue with the inspector and ask if there is an alternative to their decision that might be resolved by holding the bus until related violation(s) are corrected. Cooperation, professional courtesy, respect, and the miracle ingredient of good communication sometimes work in the agency's favor.

On the final inspection report, the MCS will cite the proper authority for the violation and/or OOS condition for either the Transportation or Maintenance Department. Regardless of the violation, it will be noted by reference document and section. For example, if Mr. X drove more than 10 hours following 8 consecutive hours off duty, the incident will be noted on the Terminal compliance report by title and section. For this example, it would be cited as 13 CCR 1212.5 (a) (1) (A). Again, the importance of having the required reference documents and knowing how to use them cannot be overemphasized.

> *Note: Not all transit bus OOS violations are covered in the CVSA, but they can be found in other reference documents discussed in previous chapters. If you cannot find a violation by title and section, contact the Terminal Host or the MCS II or III for assistance.*

The CHP Safety Compliance Bus Inspection

Inspection items that are found to exceed their Maximum Allowable limit or that may present a safety risk on the road to include driver Hours-of-Service requirements and records, are identified with an asterisk ("*") in the following three lists. Related issues will most likely render the bus Out-of-Service and/or the driver ineligible to operate a commercial vehicle. The inspectors generally are interested only in safety-related issues; however, at any time they may inspect or operate any bus component. On one occasion an MCS requested a mechanic to cycle a wheelchair lift. Knowing him professionally for many years, I intentionally reminded him that the lift was not part of the safety compliance inspection and I wanted to know his intent for cycling the lift. He simply stated, "Because it's there." In a humorous way I share this short story with you to say they will inspect and operate any/all bus related systems and components to ensure they are safe—simply because they can. And there's no law that says you can't engage in a bit of levity with the MCSs during the inspections. In moderation, it may serve a good purpose and may help cultivate a good relationship.

> *Note: A bus or any other commercial vehicle can be rendered Out-of-Service or in violation for being unsafe for a wide variety of reasons. If a safety condition exists and no specific authority can be found against it, the inspector may cite CVC §24002 Vehicle Not Equipped or Unsafe. The authority states in (a), "It is unlawful to operate any vehicle or combination of vehicles which is in an unsafe condition, or which is not safely loaded," and in (b), "It is unlawful to operate any vehicle or combination of vehicles which is not equipped as provided in this code."*

The MCS inspection involves both interior and exterior elements.

Interior inspection:

- Examine the registration/proof of ownership.
- Review the driver vehicle inspection report (pre-trip) card for date, signature, and any and all equipment violations.
- Activate the windshield wipers in all motor speeds and inspect the blades.
- Check defroster ventilation operation and motor speeds, and check vents for obstruction.*
- Check instrument panel lights and dimmer switch.
- Check air system buildup time by applying brakes to reduce pressure to 85 psi, activate fast idle, and record the time to build-up air to governor cut-out. One minute maximum.*
- Check low air pressure warning systems alarm and light operation. Ascending, alarm and light deactivate at 75–85 psi. Descending, alarm and light activate between 85 and 75 psi. Note CVSA.*
- Check back-up alarm.
- Inspect driver side window for operation and integrity.
- Check static air loss. With engine off, apply parking brake and release service brake. Maximum allowable air loss is 2 psi per minute. Note CVSA.*

- Check applied air loss. Release parking brake and fully apply service brakes. Maximum 3 psi air loss per minute. Note CVSA.*

- Inspect driver seat, adjustments, restraints, sun visors, and windshield shade.

- Check horn operation (CVC §27000) and button securement.*

- Check steering wheel and tilt adjustment. Steering wheel must operate smoothly from "stop to stop" without binding or emitting any unusual noise. Tilt adjustment must be noise free and the lock detents solid.

- Check steering wheel for maximum allowable free play. Note CVSA.*

- Inspect mirrors for proper mounting and visibility.

- Floor and coverings must be firm throughout and not present a trip hazard.

- Rear-door emergency release must be secured, hammer and glass must be intact, and release cables must operate properly.

- Operate front door and inspect for proper action, securement, rubber door seal/gap, and glass. Check door lights for illumination.

- Check rear-door operation for speed (open and close within approximately 2.5 seconds). Check door alarm and light for illumination. Sensitive edges must activate and begin to open using a 1-inch-diameter smooth cylinder device, as cited in 13 CCR 1267 (A) (iii). If both sensitive edges are non-operational, the bus will be rendered Out-of-Service. Check rear-door brake and accelerator interlock systems for proper operation.*

- Parking brake operation.
- Interlock systems must operate for wheelchair lift and kneel-function activation.*
- Inspect windshield for integrity and for "line of sight" obstruction.*
- Check windows, emergency windows, and latches for securement and damage.
- Inspect seat inserts and frames/mounting for proper securement and any damage.
- Check interior dome lights for proper operation and illumination.
- Inspect roof emergency escape hatches for proper operation and securement with proper decal identification.
- Check rear-seat engine access panel/door for securement and any missing or loose bolts.*
- Check vertical and horizontal stanchions for securement and any sharp edges.
- Inspect fire extinguisher for securement, proper charge, hose, and date tag. Note 13 CCR §1242 (c), for 5-mile-radius exception rule and NFPA 10, Chapter 8.

Violation probably will result in Out-of-Service condition.

Exterior inspection:

- Verify that CA Number decals appear on both sides of the bus.

- Check reflectors for proper securement and verify that lenses are free of obstruction.

- Inspect for the presence of bus number and carrier name on the vehicle.

- Check exterior lighting operation, including high and low headlight beams, tail lights, directional signals, marker lights, license-plate light, and reverse lights and brake lights. Note CVSA, Part 2 Lighting Devices.*

- Check exterior mirrors for proper securement, condition of mirror, and operation if powered.

- Inspector may operate the bike rack and will check for proper securement.

- Check front and side compartment doors for securement, locks, and operation. The inspector requires that the door locks properly secure the doors as designed.

- Closely inspect tires for tread depth and for any sidewall (casing) damage, which may include bubbles, cuts, and/or signs of sidewall separation. "Skidding" a tire, otherwise known as checking the tread depth, is performed with a tire-tread depth gage in 32nds of an inch. The inspectors are using their senses when inspecting tires: ears for hearing audible air leaks, eyes for identifying the smallest cuts and sidewall tears and separation, and touch for feeling escaping air in difficult-to-reach areas and for foreign objects embedded in the sidewall or tread. A tire that contacts or can be made to contact any component, as in turning the wheels "from stop to stop" that hits, for example, a brake chamber airline, is cause for an OOS. Note CVSA, Part 2 Tires.*

- Inspect rims and axle studs for cracks and torque. Axle-to-hub area is inspected for signs of oil fouling. Moderate to excessive oil is a good indicator that the brake-block-friction material is contaminated.

- Check for fuel type decal/labeling. Note NFPA 52, Vehicular Fuel System Code.

- Open the engine compartment door and inspect the engine and related components for fouled lines and hoses and worn/cracked drive belts. Verify that belt guards are secured and that tensioners operate properly. Check for exhaust, oil and fuel leaks, loose components, missing nuts and bolts, and worn motor mounts. Carefully inspect the electrical wires for chaffing and terminal blocks for securement. Where appropriate, verify that the wires at or near high-heat areas are well insulated from the heat source. Wire securement, integrity, and insulation are especially important with LNG and CNG powered vehicles.*

* Violation probably will result in Out-of-Service condition.

Undercarriage Inspection:

- Inspector will direct the mechanic to rotate the steering wheel from left to right until "steering stops" are contacted with each pass. While this is occurring, the MCS is looking for tire sidewall damage and fouling, steering gear box movement (if visible), loose pitman arm, loose pinch clamps, and excessive movement under steering load for tie rods and drag links. Vertical motion of ball-and-socket joints must not exceed 1/8 inch, measured with palm pressure. Kingpins are inspected for excessive and/or erratic movement, unusual noise, and inadequate lubrication. Note CVSA Part II Steering Mechanisms.*

- Inspect radius rods and bushings for damage and for loose, broken, bent, cracked, or worn bushings. Signs of rust at bushing areas are generally not OOS but must be adjusted or repaired if necessary.

- Carefully inspect the brake drum and disc brake rotors for OOS conditions. Note CVSA Part II under Brake Drums and Rotors.*

- Inspect disc brake pads for missing pads, oil or grease fouling, and pad thickness. Rotors that show evidence of metal-to-metal contact will render the bus Out-of-Service.*

- Carefully inspect the cam-activated type brakes for loose lining segments, brake rod travel, poor lining condition and thickness, oil/grease fouling, missing or broken lining, or exposed fasteners. Cracks that exceed 1/16 inch in width or that exceed 1-1/2 inches in length are not compliant. Note CVSA Part II Brake Systems.*

- Check brake line hoses for chaffing, exposed cord, or air leakage with brakes applied. Inspect brake chamber diaphragms for air leaks.*

- Carefully examine the air ride beams and engine and transmission frame members and steering geometry/positioning parts and component members for vertical and horizontal cracks or loose and/or sagging components. Note CVSA Part II, Suspension and Frames.*

- Check for liquid fuel systems with a dripping leak or significant saturation of fuel. (Either will render the bus OOS.) Carefully inspect CNG and LNG tanks, high pressure lines, valves, pressure relief devices, and regulators. MCSs typically use their senses to inspect gaseous powered vehicles: ears for detecting fuel leaks and eyes for identifying frosting of lines and related components. Refer to CVSA Part II Fuel Systems and *NFPA 52 Vehicular Gaseous Fuel System Code* for compliance information.*

- Ensure that bus exhaust systems powered by non-gasoline engines, to include CNG and LNG, do not emit fumes 15 inches forward of the rearmost part of the bus. Note CVSA Part II Exhaust Systems.*

- Inspect universal joints for vertical movement, measured by palm pressure not to exceed 1/8 inch. Missing or loose joint bearing caps and/or missing or loose securement bolts are non-compliant. Ensure that bearings are lubricated. Refer to CVSA Part II Universal Joint for compliance.*

Violation probably will result in Out-of-Service condition.

The buses selected for the technical inspection are automatic candidates for vehicle records inspection. The MCS will review the scheduled and unscheduled preventative maintenance (PM), related maintenance repair work cards or electronic work orders, brake reline activities, and other work that occurred on the buses within the preceding 2 or 3 months. Scheduled work such as preventative maintenance inspections will be inspected against the agency's established program at the designated mileage intervals. Typically, the CHP allows a 10 percent variance, over or under, the established mileage. Exceeding the variance either way will result in a violation for each PM on the Safety Compliance Report. Excessive violations for PM mileage can result in an Unsatisfactory Terminal Rating and point to unfavorable trends that may show inconsistencies in the maintenance program, a lack of or improper supervision, and possibly unsafe equipment.

The MCS will inspect the records for each bus to assess if the documentation is complete, properly dated, and signed by the mechanic and supervisor and that the agency is following its own program, which is expected to be effective, safe, and compliant.

The inspector also may review a random sample of mechanic CDL and medical certificates to check for any/all suspensions, citations, or expired licenses or medicals. If problems are identified, the inspector may request the agency to produce more CDL activity history on mechanics to determine if there are problems associated with the agency's Pull-Notice Program.

> *Note: On a monthly basis the Division Maintenance Manager should review, or ask the agency's Driver License Monitoring System/Pull-Notice Coordinator to review, a random sample of CDLs and medicals at the division(s).*

Last, the MCS may request, as part of the inspection, to review the Proficiency requirement on a sample number of mechanics. With few exceptions, most drivers of a commercial vehicle must have demonstrated they are capable of safely operating all new equipment, different types of buses, and/or BIT vehicles they may drive at the agency. The inspector may ask to review the physical record of training for any driver selected. The employee Proficiency record shall reflect the training received by vehicle type, controls, gages, equipment, and configuration before a driver can operate on the road unsupervised.

The amount of time required to familiarize the driver with the new piece of equipment under the law depends on the intricacies of the bus or vehicle and the amount of time the driver may need to spend behind the wheel. There is no mandatory amount of training time referenced under the Proficiency regulations; however, it is required, and the individual's training record must reflect his/her name and badge number, training covered, total training time, and activity completion date, as referenced in the following example of an employee proficiency record for CDL holders:

Employee Proficiency Document

Employee Name: John Doe Smith

Title: Bus driver

Badge Number: 05525

Location: Division 14

Training	Instruction time	Training completion date
New bus	1 Hour	September 4, 2015

The Proficiency record may be presented in either manual or electronic format. Regardless of format, the inspector will inspect, at his or her discretion, a representative number of files. *Authority cited: 13 CCR §1229 Driving Proficiency.*

The size of your fleet will determine the number of inspectors used for the Terminal review. If there are multiple MCSs, one may leave the bus inspection early and go to the Transportation Department to continue the audit.

Before the audit begins, ask the inspector(s) how they intend to inspect both Maintenance and Transportation, the number of days they may work at the agency, and if they'll be including other inspections like Drug and Alcohol, Pull Notice, and/or BIT during their audit.

If the audit is announced, you will be informed of their intentions regarding the types of inspections scheduled and inspection plan, which should give you adequate time to prepare and initiate simple bus-related campaigns to check items such as fuel leaks, lights, tire tread, air leaks, and brake pad thickness. Being rated Unsatisfactory for an announced Terminal inspection should never happen!

When the inspector(s) indicate they're ready to start with Transportation, I recommend they be escorted, especially if it's a new inspector. They may not be familiar with the location and office areas, and they would be unaware of any requirement for personal protection equipment if required. Large-size transit facilities can be confusing, and locating offices may be time consuming. Take the inspector(s) to Transportation, introduce them to the appropriate personnel, and remain available throughout the inspection.

The next chapter covers the components of the Transportation Department Terminal inspection.

8

CHP Terminal Inspection: Transportation Department

Authority cited: CVC §34501 Matters Regulated

Like Maintenance, the Transportation Department is also required by the Department of the California Highway Patrol to submit to an annual Compliance Terminal Inspection. Most often both inspections are conducted, evaluated, and Rated within the same day. And though not significant in any way, the Transportation side of the inspection typically follows the Maintenance Department audit or may be performed simultaneously if multiple inspectors are available.

The Transportation Manager or designee should have met the inspectors upon their arrival, most likely at the Maintenance Department. At that time, the Transportation representative should ask the MCSs the time they can be expected, the information they want presented, and the inspection sample size.

At mid to large transits, the sample size of the information shown in the following bullet list of inspection criteria is generally 15%; with small transits, it's more like 50–75%. For example, at a division with approximately 200 drivers, they will inspect, at the 15% level, 30 driver CDLs, 30 Proficiency checks, and any other records they request. At a very small agency with approximately 25 drivers or fewer, and to acquire a fair representative sample of the driver documents, a larger sample size is required by the CHP to determine if the programs are compliant and properly managed. The inspector will generally follow the MCS policy regarding sample size, but they are authorized to increase or decrease the size accordingly.

When the inspectors report to Transportation, they will review and evaluate the overall compliance of the related documents and other information from a sample size, generally based on the number of drivers assigned to the division. Depending on the condition of the records, logbooks, and other documents and the number of violations identified, the inspector may increase the sample size to determine if there is a pattern. Similarly, if few or no violations are found in a specific area of review, they may cease and move on with the next part of the inspection.

The components of and the inspection items for the Transportation audit, required by law, are as follows:

- CDL/medical certificates
- Pull-Notice
- Endorsements
- Verification of Transit Training
- Pre-trip cards/requirements
- Record of duty status (Hours-of Service)
- 8/80 rule
- Drive-time rule
- On-duty time rule
- Driving Proficiency
- Driver logs (if required)
- Secondary employment

Public transit drivers operate different bus types to transport their patrons to and from various locations, day or night, in inclement weather, often times in congested traffic and through gridlock conditions. They are responsible for the continued safety of their passengers while taking fares, operating wheelchair lifts and platforms, announcing stops and, might I add, to just drive the bus in revenue service. These professionals are a special breed and deserve high praise for the work they perform. For that level of responsibility, it is no wonder their profession is highly regulated, requires total compliance, and is a vital component of the CHP annual Compliance Terminal Inspection, with emphasis on general driving requirements, which are discussed in this chapter.

When the MCSs arrive at Transportation, the person assigned to present the requested information must ask them how they want to begin and what data is to be presented in whatever order or by category. There is no formal process of inspection priority or significance, as the MCSs will typically set the tone and pace for the inspection. What will change the inspection tone is if trends begin to appear regarding issues like excessive drive time or on-duty time, expired CDL and/or medical certificates, or missing logbooks, to name a few.

> *Note: Before the inspectors arrive, prepare a location where they will be comfortable while inspecting numerous documents, forms, and even procedures. The area should have a table large enough to accommodate reference books, forms, and binders, and it should have at least four chairs. It should be well lit and reasonably clean, and the room temperature, if possible, should be set to a comfortable level. At medium- to large-sized transits, the inspection of logbooks, records, files, and other documents may take a few hours, so be mindful that a small and confined area can become uncomfortable very quickly. If possible, secure a larger area, rather than a smaller one. Also, providing coffee and water is a professional courtesy. It is easy on the budget and demonstrates division pride and hospitality that will be appreciated by all who participate in the review.*

The remainder of this chapter describes the various types of general driving requirements and regulations.

CDL/Medical Certificate

By law, bus drivers are required to operate their vehicles in possession of a current CDL, medical certificate, and passenger endorsement. The MCS will nearly always inspect a large representative sample of driver CDLs and medical certificates at each location for compliance. If for any reason a license is not current or has been suspended or revoked and/or the medical certificate is invalid, the operator cannot drive and will immediately be removed from service until the issue(s) are resolved. The inspectors consider all CDL violations serious, and instances of this nature, by specific violation, will be noted on the compliance report.

Although it is uncommon for a public transit bus driver to be found with an invalid or suspended CDL and/or expired medical certificate, the problems are typically resolved within a few days, and company policy and/or the union bargaining agreement will dictate the status of the driver during that time. Again, drivers found operating in service with an invalid CDL/medical certificate must immediately be removed from service.

Verification of Transit Training (VTT)

Transit training is required of drivers who operate transit buses, as cited in the Education Code §40085.5, authority found towards the back of the *California Vehicle Code*. The inspector will audit VTT driver records to determine if they meet the annual 8-hour training requirement. The law does not dictate the exact type or content of transit training to satisfy the language of the 8-hour rule. Rather, the section suggests that training is acceptable if it's related to passenger safety, current law and procedures, accident prevention under defensive driving, passenger loading and unloading, and/or any type of training directly related to bus operations.

Since there is no stipulation regarding time for any segment of training, almost all time spent in transportation/bus related safety meetings, refresher courses or training offered through independent sources also satisfies the 8-hour requirement.

Bus Pre-Trip Inspection

Based on 13 CCR §1215 (a), the driver of a commercial vehicle must ensure it is safe to operate and properly equipped, sufficient to satisfy the legal requirements and to determine that the bus parts and accessory items are in good working order as designed by the manufacturer. Every driver who operates the bus must perform his or her pre-trip inspection.

For one individual to perform pre-trip inspections on numerous buses for a morning or afternoon pull-out, otherwise known as staging, is illegal. 13 CCR §1215 (1) clearly states that before driving a motor vehicle, in this case a bus, the "driver shall" inspect each vehicle daily; and then it continues with the required inspection items contained in the next bulleted list. Further, if a driver operates multiple buses in a work period, that driver must perform a pre-trip inspection on each bus to comply with the intent of the requirement. And though the regulations are silent on the amount of time required/allowed by California transit agencies to perform a pre-trip inspection, the average time is about 10 minutes.

13 CCR §1215 (c) stipulates, at a minimum, the pre-trip inspection items required before a bus can enter revenue service. The following items must be inspected and reported in writing, and the record must be maintained for three months, as cited in 13 CCR §1234 (e):

- Service brakes, including trailer brake connections, if applicable
- Parking (hand) brake
- Steering mechanisms
- Lighting devices and reflectors
- Tires
- Horns
- Windshield wipers
- Rear-vision mirrors
- Coupling devices
- Wheels and rims
- Emergency equipment

Note: For the public transit operator, compliance language for in-service (relief) pre-trip inspection is silent. However, it is commonly accepted that at relief, a "walk around" inspection, typically taking a few minutes, satisfies the language of 13 CCR §1215 Vehicle Condition (pre-trip inspection).

Occasionally during the Terminal inspection, the MCS will review varying numbers of pre-trip cards to determine if the inspections occurred and whether violations were noted and properly dated and signed by the driver. Often inspectors will request that the Maintenance Department provide them with the repair card(s) so they can determine if the corrective actions to the driver write-ups are occurring.

Driver Hours-of-Service Regulations

Your agency values the safety of its drivers, customers, and all other operators on the road, and I'm sure safety and compliance are its number one priority. But a major factor impacting the ability to drive safely, aside from alcohol and drug use, is driver fatigue, which is directly attributed to many highway and road-related crashes that, nationwide, result in serious injury and death. Studies have linked driver fatigue and sleep deprivation to many traffic accidents and injuries of all types.

To diminish related incidents and to help prevent drivers from having fatigue-related accidents, laws have been enacted to ensure they have appropriate off-duty time to recover from the natural effects of driving for long periods. The transit bus driver Hours-of-Service requirements are cited in 13 CCR §1212 through §1214 and will be discussed in detail in this section.

California bus drivers are operating intrastate commercial vehicles, which require the driver to be on a *service logbook*, also known as a *log, logbook,* or *grid graph*. Based on 13 CCR §1213, operators must record their duty status in duplicate for each 24-hour period. See Figure 2.

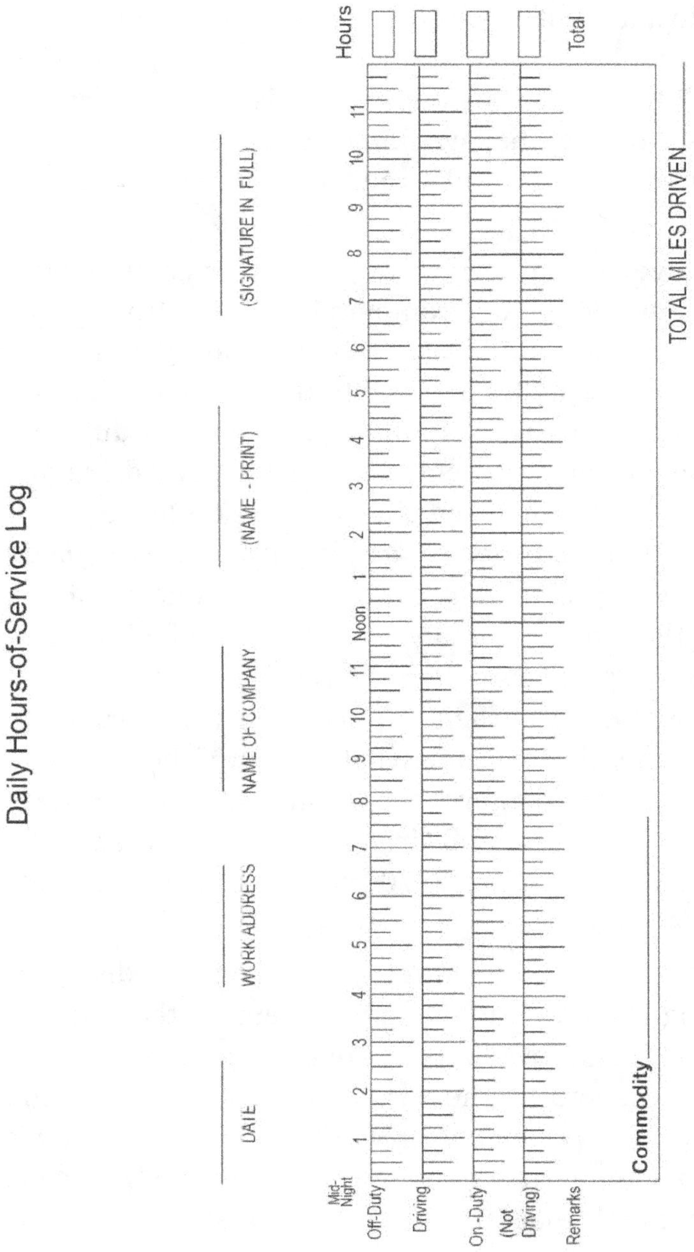

Figure 2. Daily Hours-of-Service log

Most transit operators knowingly or unknowingly have exercised an exemption as cited in 13 CCR §1212 (e) that states a driver is exempt from the requirement of the law, filing a daily log, if they operate within a 100 air-mile radius of their normal work reporting location.

However, the intrastate public transit driver under the exemption is not completely exempt from generating a logbook should they have secondary employment or exceed 12 hours of on-duty time. As cited in 13 CCR §1213 (2) (d), the location of the change of duty status (secondary employment) shall include any drive or on-duty not-drive time and city and state on the log. *Simply, if the driver has secondary employment, a logbook is required when driving a transit bus.* And chances are good that some or many of your part-time bus drivers are employed elsewhere, often operating regulated equipment. And their Hours-of-Service, particularly drive time, become somewhat unclear if they cross state lines, which renders them an interstate operator. Questions regarding a driver on interstate status and the 8/80 versus the 7/70 rule should be directed to your Motor Carrier Specialist.

Some transits require their drivers to disclose, in writing, their secondary employment, or they may have a policy that prohibits secondary employment altogether. Generally, the inspectors will ask how many drivers are on logbooks, how many have secondary employment, and how it is determined/tracked. I recommend that transits big and small have their drivers disclose all secondary employment at least once or preferably twice each year in writing, and that they keep these documents in a binder for easy access. During the audit, the MCS will review driver Hours-of-Service specifically for drive time and all on-duty time. If they find a driver who has exceeded 12 hours of on-duty time, they will most likely ask to review the log.

Before the logbook is discussed in specific detail, you must clearly understand the Hours-of-Service rules as they apply to the California public transit bus driver, as cited in 13 CCR §1212 through §1212.5, as follows:

Bus Driver Hours-of-Service Rules

Following are the driver Hours-of-Service rules:

- **10-hour rule:** Operators of transit buses must not drive more than 10 hours except for adverse driving conditions, which allows an additional 2 hours as cited in 13 CCR §1212 (b) (1). Adverse driving conditions defined include but are not limited to snow, sleet, fog, adverse weather conditions, and unusual road and traffic conditions.

- **12-hour rule:** Drivers must file a completed logbook when they exceed 12 hours of on-duty time and remain in revenue service; assuming they have not exceeded the 10 hour drive-time limit.

- **15-hour rule:** Operators must not drive a bus after having been on duty for 15 hours without 8 consecutive off-duty hours before once again operating a bus.

- **8/80 Rule:** Bus operators shall not drive after accumulating 80 hours within 8 consecutive days, including secondary employment on-duty and drive time.

During the Terminal inspection, the MCS will review driver Hours-of-Service reports for any violations and note them for exceeding time requirements on the compliance report. Excessive violations for missing logs, logs filed improperly, drivers exceeding the 10-hour rule or any other rule violation may be cause for an Unsatisfactory Terminal Rating.

> Note: If there are drivers on logbooks, it is recommended that all the logs, by day and date, be kept in a binder for quick access and review. Similarly, another binder should be maintained exclusively for drivers with reported secondary employment. Maintaining the information within binders is not required by law, but it is helpful for quick review and generally appreciated by the MCSs when it is presented in easy-to-read binder format.

Driver Record of Duty Status (the Log Book)

Authority cited: 13 CCR §1213

When required, the driver logbook (see Figure 2) serves to record operator duty status, including drive time, on- and off-duty time, total miles driven within a 24-hour period, and general information regarding the operator and the carrier. Log entries shall be made by the driver and must be legible and in the driver's handwriting. Any and all edits to the log must be made by the driver who filed it.

Note: There is no legal requirement that a driver shall be paid extra to complete a logbook.

All duty time shall be recorded on the log within the grid graph, as seen in Figure 2. In addition to the information necessary on the grid, the following is required by law on all log entries:

- Date
- Total miles driven within a 24-hour period
- Bus number
- Name of company/carrier
- Driver signature
- Address (division/depot)
- Remark section (shown in Figure 2.)
- Total hours by activity within a 24-hour period (right side of log)
- Commodity (passengers)

Log book entries are scrutinized very carefully by the MCS during the inspection. Total hours of duty must be accurate, layover time (non-drive time) must reflect city and state in the remark section, the grid and log entries must be legible, and the total miles driven must reflect the distance driven, typically taken from the odometer. In the event the odometer is non-operational, calculate the "run" mileage from the "running board or paddle" for that line, and add the calculated total mileage in the mileage driven section on the log. Make every attempt to calculate and input the miles driven, rather than leaving the section blank or notated "odometer non-operational."

All entries into the logs, specifically the grid graph, must be accurate and legible for the inspectors or any other authority that requires the information. Logs are legal documents that have been and will continue to be used in courts of law, in arbitrations, and for settling litigation. They are extremely important, and they must be accurate, concise, legible, and readily available.

Divisions have received Unsatisfactory Terminal Ratings for incomplete, missing, false, and inaccurate logbooks. Again, all entries on the log shall be made exclusively by the drivers and in their own handwriting, as cited in 13 CCR §1213 (g) (2).

Driver Proficiency Record

As discussed in Chapter 7 and as cited in 13 CCR §1229, driver Proficiency records are required of all CDL holders. Typically the MCS will inspect approximately 15% of the assigned drivers at the division. With very few exceptions, most drivers of a commercial vehicle must have demonstrated they are capable of safely operating all new equipment and different types of buses they will drive. And unlike mechanics, the bus operators do not drive BIT vehicles, so no Proficiency record is needed.

The record must reflect the training received by vehicle type, controls, gages, and equipment, as well as by configuration, before bus drivers can operate on the road unsupervised. As stated previously, there is no required amount of training time referenced in the regulations. At the mid to larger size transits that receive new buses at a division and where many drivers are assigned, I recommend the following to satisfy the language of the law and to expedite the process.

Assemble as many drivers as possible on the bus, as can be afforded. Explain/discuss the different controls, gages, and any other special equipment that may be different to them than on the older buses. Follow-up with a question-and-answer exercise and, if necessary, have the driver(s) demonstrate, if requested, the safe operation (driving) of the bus. Since training time is not referenced in the requirement, larger groups will expedite the process. And unlike what some think, the familiarization process to a driver for a new bus or a new series bus does not require small-group instruction.

Chapter 7 contains an example of an employee Proficiency record/file. This is the type of document that may be presented to the inspector in either manual or electronic format.

Secondary Employment List

A formal list identifying individuals with secondary employment of drivers is not required by law; however, the inspector will probably ask how many drivers currently have secondary employment and what mechanism the division uses to document the information. If an agency is not tracking secondary employment, it should. I recommend the division ask each driver twice a year, for example, in June and December, and file the information in either a binder or in their personnel file. The binder method is well received by the inspectors, and having these documents in one place is easy and provides a quick reference.

Overall Terminal Rating

After both departments have been inspected, the MCSs will begin writing the compliance report. The inspection findings, if any, to be reported will include, but not be limited to, the overall maintenance program, which includes brakes, lamps and signals, steering and suspension, tires and wheels, and records. Hold buses are typically identified with an asterisk, and noted in the "Remarks" section as Out-of-Service by appropriate reference document, title, and section. From among the representative sample, 20% of hold buses may constitute an overall Unsatisfactory Terminal Rate. Similarly, unacceptable driver records, to include logbooks (if applicable), VTT, and Proficiency, will be reported and may contribute to an unfavorable Rate. Driver Hours-of-Service violations that reach 5% or greater will almost always result in an Unsatisfactory Terminal Rate, regardless of how well Maintenance performed. As previously stated, problematic issues with either department will create complications for all.

The Terminal Rate is determined from the division's overall compliance with applicable laws and regulations governing the bus maintenance program/vehicle condition, driver training, Hours-of-Service, applicable department records as required by law, and number of Out-of-Service and driver violations. The Rate is determined based on the condition of the equipment, driver status, and their records—not by friendships or a long-standing relationship with the agency. Should an agency disagree with the Terminal Rate, an appeal process can be requested through the MCS III.

9

Basic, Triennial, Pull-Notice, and Drug and Alcohol Audits

The Basic Program

The California Commercial Motor Vehicle Safety Act of 1988 is better known in the bus transit industry, as of now, as The Basic Inspection of Terminal (BIT). Until January 2016, the Basic program was known as the Biennial Inspection of Terminal by the California State Legislature. The intent of the BIT is to reduce truck/equipment crashes on our roadways and to help prevent injury and death. *The required Biennial inspection audit that was conducted by the CHP Motor Carrier Team has been discontinued.* BIT inspections may now occur after crash events or if the CHP or another enforcement agency directs an inspection or investigation of non-revenue equipment, while the mandatory inspection is no longer required by law every 2 years.

Many public transit agencies utilize BIT vehicles to support their daily operation for purpose of transporting parts, Facility Department repair vehicles, revenue transport trucks, response vehicles, and tow trucks, to name a few. Types of equipment subject to BIT are found in CVC §34500 as follows:

- Any motortruck with three or more axles having a gross vehicle weight rating of more than 10,000 pounds
- Truck tractors
- Trailers or semitrailers used in combination with the vehicles listed above
- Any motortruck with a gross vehicle weight rating of more than 10,000 pounds while towing any trailer or semi-trailer that results in a combination length of 40 feet

The intent of the BIT inspection, when it occurs, is to ensure that the equipment, equipment records, driver records, and maintenance program are determined to be in compliance with Motor Carrier Safety Regulations. Your agency could receive a composite Terminal Rating based on a representative sample of the equipment, the maintenance program, the records, and the driver requirements. After the inspection, the MCS will issue your program a Rating of either Satisfactory or Unsatisfactory. Should it be rated Unsatisfactory, the facility will be re-inspected within 120 days.

Like the bus Terminal audit, the MCS will inspect to ensure that the vehicles/trailers and other related equipment are equipped as required, maintained in good working order, properly documented, and safe for operation on the road.

Transit agencies that operate equipment under the BIT program are required to inspect each vehicle and trailer within a 90-day interval, or more frequently to ensure their safe operation. The regularly scheduled 90-day inspection should include a systematic review, general maintenance, and lubrication. Based on commercial vehicle law, the following inspection activities are required, in addition to the agency's general service program, as referenced in CVC §34505.5, at intervals of no longer than 90 days:

BIT-Required Maintenance Inspection Activities

Non-revenue equipment that falls under a BIT program must be inspected, at a minimum, for the following maintenance-related systems:

- Brake adjustment
- Brake systems components and leaks
- Steering and suspension systems
- Tires and wheels
- Vehicle connecting devices

BIT vehicles shall be pre-tripped every time and by each operator before being driven on any roadway. Title 13 CCR §1215 (1) states the *driver shall* (each individual driver) perform a pre-trip inspection of the vehicle to determine if it's in safe operating condition. It is believed by some that once a vehicle is inspected it can be driven by multiple drivers throughout the day or night without an inspection by each succeeding driver. Not true and not legal!

The required pre-trip inspection shall include but not be limited to the following, as required by 13 CCR §1215 (c):

1. Service brakes, including trailer-brake connections
2. Parking (hand) brake
3. Steering mechanisms
4. Lighting devices and reflectors
5. Tires
6. Horn
7. Rear vision mirrors
8. Coupling devices
9. Wheels and rims
10. Emergency equipment

A pre-trip card is required to be completed and filed by each driver at the end of each day. A single card designed for use by multiple drivers is commonly used in the industry and is legal. That is, contrary to the belief that one card is required for each driver, a single card with multiple entries is legally acceptable. The cards represent a lawful document and shall be maintained at the garage or division for a minimum of 3 months. The BIT driver is also required to comply with driver Proficiency as cited in 13 CCR §1229, wherein he/she has demonstrated the ability to safely and properly operate the equipment.

Interestingly, many Maintenance Managers and Division Supervisors who have attended my compliance training are completely unaware of the requirements of BIT, and what the law expects from the motor carrier. According to the *California Vehicle Code*, BIT equipment is a commercial vehicle and must be maintained and serviced and have proper records management, and the driver must follow all applicable general driving requirements. Should an unfortunate incident occur that involves injury and/or fatality, it will be investigated like any other commercial vehicle. Following any major incident, one of the first of many actions will be to request the 90-day BIT inspection records, pre-trip reports, and the driver's Pull-Notice history.

I strongly recommend that, on a yearly basis, staff inspect and evaluate their BIT program against the legal requirements and perform in-house simulated inspections of the equipment, records, driver license status, Pull-Notice, and Proficiency records. Senior management must be copied on any/all simulated inspections and informational reports. If necessary, contact your CHP Host (the primary contact assigned to your facility) for assistance if your program requires additional evaluation and further improvement. This is not a warning but a wooing; as I've said before, it's easier to ask for assistance from the MCSs to identify program inadequacies before they find deficiencies (if any) upon an inspection, if and when required.

Within Maintenance, the BIT program or the preventative maintenance activities may not be clearly understood because of the fog of the bus business (many pressing issues and challenges). The trucks and trailers, as well as other miscellaneous equipment, maintenance, and repairs, can sometimes fall through the proverbial cracks because of the relentless demand to make timely bus pull-outs. Maintenance Managers, do yourselves a favor. If you don't have a BIT Coordinator or assigned person to manage the non-revenue fleet, assign someone the responsibility now. Have that person report to you on a quarterly basis regarding the status of BIT maintenance, pre-trip inspections, records retention, and all Matters Regulated; then you can take action if required.

BIT inspections are measured and Rated against applicable laws and regulations gleaned from the inspection results. The inspection outcome provides a mechanism for determining the program effectiveness and vehicle safety, and it provides management with useful information for future planning and funding of the non-revenue department/program. As with a bus, an Unsatisfactory Rating will result in a re-inspection within 120 days.

The Triennial Audit

The Triennial safety compliance audit is performed once every 3 years—not by the CHP but rather by an independent transit professional audit group. The inspections are required of public transits that receive state and federal funding. They are nearly always announced well in advance to give the agency ample time to gather related documents, assign in-house departmental representatives, and prepare a plan to present a quality performance. The audit is comprehensive; it may require a few weeks to conduct (depending on transit size) and will involve the collection of much data from many departments within the agency.

While a Triennial audit is required and important, it also provides an opportunity for an objective and comprehensive review of the agency's programs, how public funds are being utilized, and for any and all efficiencies and effectiveness of departmental activities. In addition, the audits provide an evaluation of the organization from an independent auditor.

Following are the major departments included in a Triennial audit:

- Facilities Maintenance
- Human Resources
- Maintenance and Transportation (similar to a CHP Terminal inspection)
- Rail (if multi-modal)
- Non-Revenue (commercial vehicles, non-bus)
- Finance
- Departments responsible for Americans with Disabilities Act and the Drug and Alcohol Program
- Administration Department (for Pull-Notices)

The Pull-Notice Program

Authority cited: CVC, §1808.1 Employer Notification

The Pull-Notice Program, also known as the Driver License Monitoring System, requires the employer of Class A, B, or C license holders with appropriate endorsements to participate in a state system that provides employers with the current public record of the driver(s) as recorded by the Department of Motor Vehicles. The information provided includes but is not limited to accidents, license suspensions or revocations, failures to appear, and/or any other record violation. Depending on the size of the agency and the number of assigned MCSs, the agency's Pull-Notice Program may be inspected the same day or the following day of a Terminal audit. Often the medium to large agency's Pull-Notice inspections will be scheduled independently. Regardless, they are almost always announced, which allows adequate time to prepare. The MCSs will ask to review a percentage of enrolled driver records and evaluate the agency's overall program and information availability.

Whenever the Pull-Notice Program is scheduled independently, it often will be combined with the annual Drug and Alcohol inspection. Regardless, the inspectors are very flexible regarding the schedule date and time.

Note: The Pull-Notice, Drug and Alcohol, Triennial, and Biennial inspections all receive independent Ratings of either Satisfactory or Unsatisfactory, unless being re-inspected for an Unsatisfactory, which generally results in a Conditional Rate.

The Drug and Alcohol Program

Authority cited: California Vehicle Code *§34520 Controlled Substances and Alcohol Use Testing and* 49 Code of Federal Regulations *Part 382 §382.103 (a) and Part 655.*

Motor Carriers and public transit operators must comply with the controlled substances and alcohol use requirements mandated by the federal government. The CHP Motor Carrier team will annually inspect and Rate the public transits to determine if their Drug and Alcohol Programs meet the requirements of federal law.

For a comprehensive and general information list for motor carriers regarding controlled substances and alcohol testing compliance, refer to the CHP 800F (form), available online. By following the checklist, a transit agency can greatly improve the likelihood to be Rated Satisfactory upon completion of the required inspection.

10

Reversing an Unsatisfactory Terminal Rate

It's unfortunate to be in the position of having to sign your "John Henry" on an Unsatisfactory CHP Safety Compliance, Terminal Inspection report, as the agency's representative accepting deficiencies such as drivers' exceeding the Hours-of-Service rules, a non-compliant fleet, or excessive Out-of-Service violations. But before I share my recommendations on how to prepare for the upcoming inspection and a generic plan for reversing the Terminal evaluation, I want to spend a moment on the pre-condition environment that most likely caused the system to fail.

First, it's important to realize that the identified problems/issues certainly did not occur overnight; rather, they were undoubtedly manifesting themselves over a long period for a variety of reasons. Towards the beginning of the book, I referenced the 30-year transit veteran who may have questioned the need to read this book, based on his/her perceived knowledge and vast experience regarding the regulations as related to a compliant system. Unfortunately, too many Maintenance and Transportation Supervisors and Managers are quicker to raise their fist up to fight than to realize they do not possess the proper skills and information base to effectively promote regulatory-driven programs and to communicate compliance requirements with CHP Motor Carrier Specialists, legal entities, and/or regulatory agencies. Further, many do not understand the legal standards of mechanical conditions from the compliance perspective; they may never have read and therefore cannot apply statutory law or applicable regulations as the fundamental basis for their programs.

For example, how can Maintenance staff ensure that the equipment is not only safe but compliant with the law if they're unfamiliar with commercial vehicle Out-of-Service criteria or the *California Code of Regulation*? What assurance do Maintenance Managers/Supervisors have that their mechanics are performing a required pre-trip inspection on a bus ready for road test, when the driver is most likely unfamiliar with 13 CCR §1215 Vehicle Condition (pre-trip)? Or, how can an agency be confident with bus drivers' filing a logbook because of secondary employment, when some staff are unaware of the requirement as cited in 13 CCR §1213 (d) Record of Duty Status? And, unless asked and documented, some transit agencies are unaware of drivers' having secondary employment.

For those reasons and many more, it is no wonder some bus Terminals are Rated Unsatisfactory for issues that are usually well within their control. Often, the problems start and continue because of a lack of knowledge of commercial vehicle law and, at times, the reliance on others to ensure that Matters Regulated are fully compliant. And typically, the higher you go within an agency, the less is known about regulatory compliance regarding equipment, records, driver requirements, and other administrative audits such as Pull-Notice and Drug and Alcohol Programs.

Unfortunately, many think that most, if not all, compliance issues are found in the Code of Federal Regulations. When confronted about the federal code by part and section, the response is typically, "you know, it's in the federal code." That baseless response, which has been shared with me often throughout my career, raises major concerns about the level of understanding of commercial vehicle law, and it will present serious problems for a transit agency regarding Terminal and ordered inspections.

Frankly, commercial vehicle training has typically been nonexistent while we've raised, through no fault of our own, a transit generation who have not been compliance trained and are inexperienced with governing law and compliance guidelines. However, we continue to make pull-out, repair buses, file the records for indiscriminate amounts of time, and do our absolute best to ensure that drivers comply with the General Driving Requirements, all with a questionable knowledge base to cite the legal authority, find the applicable reference documents, or accurately connect the regulatory dots. Amazing! Even worse, few agencies possess a complete and current set of the commercial vehicle compliance reference documents.

It is reasonable to want to trust our supervisors, mechanics, drivers, file clerks, schedulers, and others to perform their job functions and responsibilities according to state and federal regulations. However, often we get into trouble simply because we "don't know what we don't know" regarding the Matters Regulated, which, when applied, will prevent undesirable audits and embarrassing moments.

In this heavily regulated and highly litigious society, we can no longer continue operating without a good understanding of the required laws and regulations that govern Maintenance, Transportation, and administrative programs. We must make decisions and manage departments based on the language and requirements of the law governing Out-of-Service requirements, maintenance practices, driver regulations, and proper records management. Failure to operate according to the regulations will result in inspection complications, expose the agency to unwarranted liability, and may result in Unsatisfactory Terminal and/or BIT inspections. Furthermore, proper compliance with applicable law is imperative regarding bus-crash events or bus-related incidents involving fatalities, injuries, and/or property damage.

Reasons for an Unsatisfactory Terminal performance are as varied as they are embarrassing and stressful. The CEO of a small transit property in greater Los

Angeles who had experienced his second Unsatisfactory Rating a few years ago told me that being rated Unsatisfactory after the Terminal inspection was one of the most unpleasant events he's experienced in his long transit career. He recently retired, and I'm certain he doesn't miss CHP Terminal audits or anything else inspected by regulatory agencies.

If your department is Rated Unsatisfactory for any reason, immediate and decisive action must occur. The following scope-of-action list is presented as recommendations to assist in reversing the unacceptable Terminal Rate.

An inspected Terminal receiving an Unsatisfactory compliance Rating will be re-inspected within 120 days after the issuance of the Rating. The bullet points are in order of descending importance; and, depending on the size of your fleet, the number of violations and the department responsible for the problems will determine the amount of recovery time necessary to prepare.

> *Note: If the re-inspected Terminal has shown satisfactory improvement in the problem areas and the overall maintenance, and driver and records management programs appear to be in compliance with applicable law, the MCSs will probably issue the agency a Conditional Rate as opposed to a Satisfactory Rate as cited in 13 CCR §1233 (3).*

Scope of action to reverse an Unsatisfactory Terminal Rate:

- After the safety compliance report has been issued and signed, immediately inform senior staff of the result and explain the 120-day re-inspection requirement by reference document and section. Communicate that a team is being selected to develop the improvement plan to resolve the identified problems and to implement programs/campaigns.

- Designate an individual, either the Maintenance or Transportation Manager, to lead the corrective action team.

- Within days, develop a team that consists of at least one person each from the Maintenance and Transportation departments, a person with compliance experience, a representative from Quality Assurance (if the position exists), and a highly competent clerk who is familiar with records management.

- Immediately convene the team, expose the issues, and begin to develop an improvement plan. Regardless of which department was primary for the Unsatisfactory Rate, the multidisciplinary team should meet weekly, until the CHP returns, to ensure that the work progresses and that the division is prepared for re-inspection. Be advised, the 120-day period will pass quickly! As such, there is no time for general reflection, pause in action, or ascertaining of blame, as all of that will certainly be determined in time.

- After the team has been established and corrective work begins, request an audience with the MCS to introduce your team and to explain the recommended actions taken to resolve any/all problems. The meeting will convey a strong signal that the Unsatisfactory Rate was taken seriously and that quick and effective change to programs (where needed) will ensue.

- If the predominant issues were equipment Out-of-Service, determine if there is a trend or if the violations were isolated. Carefully review the inspection findings for type and number of instances, define the problems, and prioritize inspection/repair campaigns on all the buses at the division.

- If the issues were Transportation related, whether logs, transit training, Hours-of-Service, or other, initiate corrective action by violated driver(s) and then inspect a good sample of the remaining drivers assigned to the division. Upon re-inspection, be prepared for the MCS to go back approximately 3 months and look at CDL/medicals, Hours-of-Service, transit training (8-hour annual requirement), logbooks (if required), some type of list for secondary employment, and pre-trip cards. The inspectors will inspect the cards for proper date, vehicle number, and signatures and to identify if violations are being noted.

   For the re-inspection, both managers and the department head/COO should corporately greet the inspectors in the morning, brief them on the actions taken, campaigns performed and any records-management adjustments that have been made to improve the division's overall performance. Before the inspection begins, explaining the work performed to the inspector(s) sends a positive message that the division is prepared for re-inspection and has worked diligently, through a detailed inspection plan, in resolving the noted areas of improvement as referenced in the compliance report. The inspectors will refer to the previous report, specifically the problem areas, and will expect to find improvement. If satisfactory improvements are noted, the division will be Rated Conditional.

Note: A reasonable and frequently asked question is whether the CHP/Motor Carrier Inspectors can close a division for an Unsatisfactory Rating. The answer is no; they do not have the authority and will not close a division for any reason, including a bad Terminal inspection or repeat Unsatisfactory performance. They do have the authority, at any time, to remove a commercial and/or non-revenue vehicle from service for vehicle violations or a driver from service based on driver-requirement violations. Should a public transit operator receive successive Unsatisfactory Ratings, the MCSs, through their department, can present the issue to the District Attorney's office for review and action, if any. I am unaware of, nor has any

MCS ever informed me of, a public transit agency/bus division's being closed for non-compliance reasons.

How to Cultivate a Good Relationship with Inspectors

As a commercial vehicle operator and as previously stated, your agency is subject to compliance inspections based on state and federal regulations. And regardless of inspection type, interval, or previous Ratings, one thing is certain: The inspections are conducted by a certified, highly trained, and knowledgeable professional who always promotes an environment of motor vehicle safety. This is done primarily through the CHP, which assists in the development of critical safety standards, proper training of new inspectors, guidance for the commercial vehicle operator to help improve their programs, and communicating new regulations.

During the course of business, your agency will be inspected for compliance, may provide information and record documentation about the condition of your fleet, driver Hours-of-Service status, records, and other regulatory-based information. Inspectors may include the CHP Motor Carrier Safety Unit, the CHP Multidisciplinary Accident Investigation Team, and possibly a third party entity contracted to perform the Triennial audit that involves activities discussed in this book, plus other inspections that are not specifically under the commercial vehicle compliance authority.

The Motor Carrier team may also be called upon to inspect your fleet and/or related records for complaints registered by a driver, a patron, or any other person who identifies a real or perceived problem they believe is unsafe or requires attention. For example, I am aware of instances where drivers, union officials, and/or patrons have contacted their local CHP office regarding issues of bus safety, equipment requirements, driver Hours-of-Service time and/or for any concern they perceive as a safety-related issue. Typically, complaints are filed for unusual and loud engine and/or transmission noise, unpleasant odors, a rough ride, loose seats, and other concerns. I specifically remember a few drivers challenging the driver Hours-of-Service regulations and the legal requirement to file logbooks for time exceeding 12 hours on-duty and the secondary employment rule. When these types of complaints are filed, they are typically submitted to the local CHP department, which tasks the Motor Carrier Team to initiate an investigation.

In this case, the MCS III, Unit Supervisor, or a designee will contact your agency and schedule an initial meeting. If you are contacted by the CHP representative, immediately inform senior management of the issue and the scheduled meeting. And regardless of how insignificant you may think the issue is, treat every complaint as serious, work openly and diligently with the inspector, and keep senior management well informed. Whatever the inspection or review that follows, it is not considered a regulated/scheduled inspection for Rating purposes, but rather a response to a registered concern.

My experience with this type of investigation has proven, in almost every instance, to be a "no defect found" condition or general "non-hold" regulatory violation. Either way, after the investigation, the inspector will communicate in writing as to how he or she will proceed with final closure. This is an informal process and related issues are typically easily resolved; but again, these matters must be properly communicated to appropriate staff. The CHP will almost always issue a final response letter to the complainant relative to its investigative actions, findings if any, and interactions with the agency.

CHP Motor Carrier Safety Unit

The Motor Carrier Safety Unit personnel work for the Department of the CHP at eight locations throughout California (see Appendix E). Staffing at each location consists of varying numbers of MCS I's, MCS II's, and the most senior person—the MCS III (Unit Supervisor), who is responsible for all elements of the team and their activities, training, and inspections, to name a few.

Contrary to what some may think, not only are the Motor Carrier Specialists a highly trained and skilled team of professionals, but they are seriously committed to the integrity of the equipment they inspect and are genuinely concerned about driver fatigue, proper records maintenance and retention, and a host of other safety-related issues.

Primarily they are inspectors of the Maintenance and Transportation Department compliance activities and are also authorized by the state legislature to inspect and Rate the Pull-Notice, Drug and Alcohol, and BIT programs for efficiency, effectiveness, and compliance. As required by law, they will inspect and Rate each of the programs accordingly. As part of the Maintenance and Transportation audits, they will inspect transit training records, CDLs, and medical certificates for violations. They will inspect logbooks, when required, and vehicle condition and will review the overall bus-maintenance program.

I cannot overemphasize the importance of having agency staff, to include middle and upper management, take a partnership role with the MCS III and his/her team, specifically regarding Matters Regulated. At many of the transits I've visited over the years, I've been told, to my surprise, that they consider the Annual Terminal inspection as simply a yearly activity they will endure for a few days, for it only to be repeated the following year. That type of attitude breeds complacency, which should not be tolerated at any agency.

To build or develop a comprehensive compliance program, management may consider the following:

- With CHP involvement, develop a well-trained compliance team.
- Make commercial-vehicle reference documents available to staff.
- Invite your Motor Carrier Specialist to the division(s) upon arrival of new buses.
- Involve shift supervisors and some "lead" people in the compliance preparedness and readiness process.
- Perform in-house simulated CHP inspections to evaluate the effectiveness of Maintenance and Transportation programs, condition of the buses, records-management programs, and driver preparedness.
- Occasionally invite the Host or the MCS III to the division to give mechanics and other related individuals an opportunity to ask compliance questions.
- Share audit results with all staff and discuss the identified violations in such a way as to bring awareness to the process.
- Celebrate Satisfactory Terminal Ratings with all staff on all shifts and occasionally invite the Motor Carrier Host.

Partner with the MCS team members with any component of the inspection(s); develop a professional relationship with the Division Host, the MCS III, and each inspector. Some inspectors remain at their Unit for years, which provides a good opportunity to develop a personal relationship and to understand their inspection style and preferences and how they individually establish the final Rating. Never harbor an attitude that your programs are always Satisfactory unless you have a Compliance Champion who updates you on a regular basis and submits scheduled, simulated inspection reports. Only then can you be somewhat assured that your programs are fully compliant and can stand the test of evaluation at any time.

> *Note: Regardless, legal discovery for information, record impound, and vehicle inspection can occur at any time, should there be a crash, major incident involving the bus, driver CDL status, or any litigation. And it is beneficial to know how the inspectors handle different issues as they occur. Generally for crash incidents involving fatalities and/or multiple injuries, the CHP Motor Carrier Team in that area will be the inspectors of the equipment and driver records.*

Inspection Activities

At the time of inspection and when requested by the MCS, ensure that all related documents are presented in titled format by someone who can articulate and clearly present the information knowledgeably and with authority. There is no required format within which to present the requested information, electronic or hard copy; but the inspector(s) must have a reasonably good comfort level that the agency has a well-defined program, properly documented, and with data readily available upon request. Accurate dates, times, and intervals, with appropriate signatories—all in an accessible file—are required and, more importantly, expected.

For the annual terminal inspection, whether it is announced or unannounced, immediately assign an accomplished mechanic with a pleasant personality to work directly with the inspector(s). Thoroughly clean the surrounding area where the buses will be inspected, and ensure that the pit or hoist area is well lit and free of trip hazards and debris. Safety is paramount for all involved in the inspection, and it is your responsibility to make sure the inspectors are comfortable and working in a safe environment. Provide them with any and all safety equipment required by your agency, for example, eye protection, gloves if requested, and bump caps.

Upon their arrival, both the Transportation and Maintenance Managers, and especially senior staff, should greet the inspectors, welcome them to the agency, and inform them they are available any time throughout the inspection. Ask them if they have any special needs or requirements, and introduce the mechanics who will be working with them throughout the day. You will be sending a powerful message that your agency is serious about compliance reviews, supports the inspection process, and is confident in the condition of the equipment and driver records.

Note : Once the inspector selects a bus, it is considered "on hold" and cannot be used for service; and at no time can a mechanic perform any type of work, repair, or adjustment, regardless of how

insignificant, on the bus without the express
approval of the inspector.

If the inspector determines a bus to be Out-of-Service, do not hesitate to ask why; and if you do not know where to find the violation in the resource documents, ask them to cite the regulatory authority by reference document and section. Remember, the inspection process is also a learning opportunity for those involved and can be an open treasure chest of valuable information if you choose to use the opportunity for the good of the agency. It is also wise to ask the inspector questions about the regulatory process, the Out-of-Service criteria, how a Terminal is Rated, or any other questions relative to commercial vehicle compliance. I assure you they do not wake up in the morning and decide which Terminals they are going to Rate Unsatisfactory for equipment-related violations, records, or general driver requirements. And contrary to some opinions within the transit community, the inspectors do not have a quota for failing Terminals or finding a specific number of Out-of-Service violations.

The larger agencies with numerous divisions should consider conducting a year-end CHP Terminal inspection meeting to discuss the agency's overall compliance performance for the year. Topics can be division Ratings, total division number of Out-of-Service violations, applauding the divisions when no defects are found, and recognizing the inspectors for their cooperative performance and continued assistance. Assuming the year was not disastrous, it can be a motivating luncheon involving representatives from the divisions, senior Maintenance and Transportation staff, and the CHP Motor Carrier Specialists, scheduled through the MCS III. It is used as an open forum to interact with the MCSs, demonstrates unity, and plays a major role in cultivating a culture of compliance. Take every opportunity to work collaboratively with and involve the Motor Carrier Team in related regulatory compliance business within your organization. Truly, they are a part of your team!

12

Developing a Culture of Regulatory Compliance

Here's a message for the Maintenance and Transportation Department Heads: If you're uncertain whether your departments are compliant based on commercial vehicle law or if they are managed by people who should be familiar with the regulations but are not capable of professionally articulating them with legal entities and regulatory experts, then you need to embark upon initiating a widespread regulatory compliance effort targeting Maintenance, Transportation, and the administrative groups responsible for the Pull-Notice and Drug and Alcohol Programs.

A foundational culture of compliance must be initiated and a plan should be developed to improve the effectiveness of maintenance programs, drivers' Hours-of-Service, and record keeping, all based on commercial vehicle laws. Staff must be thoroughly trained on the law specific to their departmental responsibilities and operation and must know how to access the information either online or by reference document. Similarly, staff who manage/oversee the Pull-Notice and the Drug and Alcohol Programs should be trained on what the law requires according to 49 CFR.

It starts with assessing your current regulatory culture and programs within both Maintenance and Transportation, identifying who is involved in Matters Regulated and at what level, and creating a new awareness of regulatory understanding and responsibility among staff. Unfortunately, many good transit employees who have worked hard throughout the years in varying capacities cannot articulate why they are doing some or many things relative to proper documentation, compliance by regulatory governance, records management, and/or the required annual inspections. Their knowledge of specifically CVSA (the Out-of-Service guide) and *Title 13, California Code of Regulation* is most likely weak at best.

Let's be honest: Your organization probably doesn't have an assigned Compliance Champion who leads the agency through Terminal inspections, audit and crash investigations, and brake and safety tests, let alone has a representative(s) who genuinely understands Matters Regulated and commercial vehicle law. And I'm certain that by now, after reading the previous chapters, you have reached the obvious conclusion that a strong and necessary compliance effort is required. The litmus test to what I've just said should be evident based simply on the results from the "test your knowledge" assessment, presented in Chapter 3.

Okay, relative to the above information, past or recent unfavorable Terminal Ratings, or the fact that you've just realized some things must change, you've decided to initiate a new and relevant regulatory compliance program. Congratulations!

Let me begin by saying that regardless of agency size, company culture, budget, past Terminal Ratings, or any other performance gage or inspection results, cultivating a regulatory-compliant agency is paramount. It will be challenging yet rewarding, organizationally new but essential for the good of the agency, and imperative to ensure consistent Satisfactory Terminal inspection Ratings and administrative audits to include the Triennial review. The decision to fashion a department-wide compliance culture will require strong leadership, a commitment from the highest level of the organization, and persistence. Just determining how and where to begin will be daunting, but with perseverance and the right team you can and will begin to connect the regulatory dots.

The benefits of the effort will validate your programs, support the need for change in some areas, document achievements, and elevate the knowledge base of many who need to understand what they do based on the appropriate language of the law while eliminating assumption and conjecture. Further, the effort will exchange archaic ways of doing business for exacting operational-based decisions supported by statutory law and regulations. The return on investment will be incalculable!

Developing a Purpose Driven Regulatory Compliance Program

In Rome there can only be one Caesar. Similarly, a transit agency, regardless of size, should have only one lead compliance person for Maintenance and Transportation and administrative reviews, responsible for ensuring that staff—from mechanic to manager, from driver to director, and including all others within the agency—understand and comply with appropriate laws. He/she should attend the Terminal and BIT inspections, accident investigations, and bus, brake and safety reviews if possible. Further, this individual should meet with and accompany the regulatory agencies and legal experts after crash and accident events, as well as outside investigators and legal counsel, to provide technical assistance and information if necessary. This person can either fill the position in a full-time capacity, depending on the size and budget of the organization, or assume the responsibility in addition to other duties. Regardless, the coordinated on-going effort must be managed, organized, and controlled through one individual, yet supported by assigned staff from other departments, which are also (I trust) being introduced to commercial vehicle law.

What is often not realized is that employees who repair or drive buses, those who file the legal records, and many supervisors, to include instructors, are responsible for complying with varying aspects of the law, specific to department function. Many have no idea they are legally responsible for their involvement with maintenance repair and service, vehicle operation, records development and management, Hours-of-Service requirements, and other activities governed by law.

Without proper oversite, effective communication, and occasional simulated in-house inspections, regulatory breeches can easily occur without notice. For example, logs may not have been prepared when required, because not all Transportation supervisors were aware of the driver Hours-of-Service rules or that secondary employment mandates the filing of a logbook. Or, often, mechanics do not perform pre-trip inspections before going on a road test after bus repairs have been made. For those and many other reasons, commercial vehicle law, the development of a new-found compliance awareness culture, and regulatory training have never been so essential.

Learn from those transit professionals who have developed good regulatory compliance behaviors and programs and who have intentionally learned how to connect vehicle maintenance and driver requirements and maintain accurate recordkeeping according to the requirements of commercial vehicle law. AC Transit in Oakland, under COO Jim Pachan and Director of Maintenance Sal Llamas, have revised their preventative maintenance program, in part, based on CVSA (the Out-of-Service guide) and are training their mechanics on the "maximum allowable" limits on bus equipment as inspected during the CHP Terminal audit and the drivers on general driver requirements. Having a well-informed staff, properly trained on commercial vehicle law, improves vehicle reliability, reduces the chance for a vehicle to be removed from service, helps prevent drivers from operating illegally, and provides staff with unquestionably accurate legal information.

In 2015, AC Transit sent numerous staff to compliance training and performed in-house audits on driver records and equipment. They are conveying the important message that individual actions are serious and their daily responsibilities may have severe regulatory consequences, based on the requirements of the law that governs their actions. They are creating a new and exciting culture of regulatory compliance, initiated and supported by senior staff members.

Los Angeles Metro has a very effective compliance program that has stood the test of thousands of bus Terminal inspections, crash investigations, BIT audits, and Pull-Notice and Drug and Alcohol Program reviews. Their successes are founded on a long-standing and strong compliance culture grounded on continued regulatory training and a resilient partnership with the Southern Division, CHP Motor Carrier Team, while performing simulated in-house inspections on the buses, records, and driver requirements. Senior staff encourage action based on regulatory compliant principles, support in-house auditing, and encourage a continued and meaningful partnership with the CHP. Los Angeles Metro requires that vehicle safety and general driver requirements be fully compliant; they communicate the need to follow and properly apply the regulations and will not settle for anything less.

They have created a robust regulatory compliance culture throughout the agency, while never under-estimating the power of change within the organization.

Recommendations

Here are several recommendations for implementing a regulatory compliance program while developing a new company culture.

➔In the interest of saving time and energy, let's assume you've decided to initiate action to develop a compliance-based program for Maintenance, Transportation, and the administrative audits for the Pull-Notice and Drug and Alcohol Programs that must always be compliant.

Through your agency's process, select an individual (Compliance Coordinator) who is capable, is reasonably familiar with the agency, can process new concepts and ideas, can convey information, and is willing to learn commercial vehicle law as listed in Appendix A, Department Pillars of Regulatory Compliance. Avoid the temptation to award the position to a person based on seniority, to a supervisor solely because he or she may have *additional* time to manage a project, or to someone who is simply "a good ol' boy" and well-liked by all. It is imperative that the person possess good writing skills and be able to effectively (verbally) communicate to staff, senior management, legal entities and regulatory enforcement personnel, and attorneys.

Last and most important, it must be understood that the effort of developing a new culture will be a continued work in progress, which necessitates the participation of many people throughout the agency, expects support from senior management, and will certainly require hard work to learn how the regulatory dots are connected and how they apply to work-related activities discussed throughout the book.

➔Immediately provide the Compliance Coordinator with the resource documents and a copy of *The Compliance Maze* and have them participate in all motor-carrier–required inspections and audits.

The Compliance Coordinator should contact the MCS Host and schedule a meeting to inform them of the recent decision to develop a defined compliance program that will be the starting point for a new company culture based on a team effort and supported by senior management for all Matters Regulated. That meeting should set the tone for a long-standing relationship that will benefit both agencies. The Motor Carrier team will undoubtedly assist in every way and be one of the primary sources for information outside the reference documents. Further, the action will convey to the CHP that they have a designated point of contact, that the transit agency is serious about improving the compliance programs, and that all Matters Regulated will be more effectively managed based on the decision to follow the law according to their authority.

Further, individuals from represented staff to senior management should be notified in writing about the decision and course of action regarding the development of the compliance program.

→Taken seriously, a new culture will emerge as management establishes its intention to advance the inspection/audit process, involve staff, and follow a course of action rooted in commercial vehicle law.

Note: A complete set of reference documents and this book should be available to all division staff at the Maintenance and Transportation Departments and those involved with the administrative reviews. The necessary reference documents and this book will cost approximately $500 in total. They will include the California Vehicle Code, Commercial Vehicle Safety Alliance, National Fire Protection Association Codes 10 and 52, Title 13 California Code of Regulation, *and* 49 Code of Federal Regulations *Parts 300 to 399, Parts 400 to 599, and Part 655.*

→The Compliance Coordinator should "benchmark" the last 2 years of Terminal and BIT inspections and the Pull-Notice and Drug and Alcohol reviews by their Ratings. All equipment Out-of-Service and driver deficiencies must be identified by violation and number of instances to determine if any trends or major problems exist. Should Unsatisfactory Ratings be identified, the coordinator must determine how the issues were resolved and when the 120-day re-inspection occurred.

Regardless of when the CHP annual inspection is due, a simulated inspection should be ordered. Simulated inspections may be performed either by representatives from an in-house Quality Assurance group or by qualified staff under the direction of the Compliance Coordinator within the different departments. Obviously, transits differ in size and staffing level, but the importance of self-inspections cannot be overemphasized. For example, the Los Angeles Metro uses representatives from its Quality Assurance group to perform simulated CHP Terminal inspections at eleven bus divisions, twice each year. A representative sample of the buses is inspected against the CVSA for Out-of-Service conditions and for general violations, while the maintenance records are reviewed for completeness, proper dates, and signatures. Similarly, driver logbooks are also inspected for accuracy and Hours-of-Service time.

Driver records are carefully scrutinized by the MCSs, and they expect to find accurate logs, if applicable, and Hours-of-Service that comply with the hourly rules. Moreover, current CDLs and medicals are another hard target. *Remember, regarding simulated in-house inspections and reviews, if things are measured then they're treasured and generally not overlooked or ignored.*

The Compliance Coordinator must also ensure that the representatives who manage the Pull-Notice and the Drug and Alcohol Programs are doing so properly, according to law. These programs are inspected annually by the Motor Carrier group and are issued a Rating based on the program performance, the records themselves, and program management according to the requirements. The Maintenance or Transportation programs are equally vulnerable to an Unsatisfactory Rating if not properly managed. Remember the woman

I referenced at the beginning of the book regarding Pull-Notice? She admitted that she had no idea where to find the legal requirements for Pull-Notice, which she was responsible for managing. That's terribly unsettling when you consider this individual was responsible for a program that tracks drivers' current public records as recorded by the Department of Motor Vehicles for (CDL) convictions, failures to appear, accidents, license revocation, and other violations.

→Communicate the compliance program, progress, and participation to staff members, from mechanic and driver to directors, on a regular basis—so often that related departments know your name and identify you as the compliance person who is not only approachable but the "go-to person" for accurate information. Honestly, commercial vehicle law is not the most exciting read; and it's challenging, if not overwhelming, for a carrier or any individual to digest the material without learning how to use the different reference documents. That's why the Compliance Coordinator must make every attempt to conduct short training/refresher sessions on all things regulated, like how to file a logbook, reminders for mechanics that pre-trips are required before road tests, the legal length of time that records must be maintained, that mechanics must understand the Out-of-Service criteria for bus-related safety compliance issues, and so on.

Regular "tailgate" training sessions focusing on regulations must be conducted in order to reinforce the business, but they also serve to reaffirm and promote the defining of the new culture—that of regulatory compliance throughout the agency. The Compliance Coordinator is responsible for communicating the requirements of the law, by reference document and section and as they relate to distinct job functions. Further, transit agencies have a responsibility to inform staff that they are directly responsible to comply with state and federal laws and regulations as they apply. Always be prepared to show the reference document, cite the authority, reveal the section, and read it out loud if possible. For that reason, it is extremely important for all responsible divisions to have updated resource documents available.

→The compliance information that is shared for any reason with staff must be readily available and should be presented upon request. Remember that, for a while, you may be the only resource to show and/or explain the law as it applies directly to their business. Managers and upper management must be regularly informed about what is being communicated, and any changes to standard operating procedures for staff should include the involvement of union representatives, if applicable.

If, for example, a transit agency determines that some drivers have secondary employment and/or exceed the 12-hour on-duty rule, the agency should begin to require logbooks, a requirement that a bar-gaining unit may challenge, especially if they were not informed of the legal requirement. Now before you say, "If logs are required by law, for whatever reason, they (unions) have no other choice but to comply," you would be correct. However, I suggest that the union(s) be involved early on to discuss the legal issues relative to compliance and their membership as they may arise, which could possibly require a change in some procedure or policy requirement of the driver or mechanic.

Over time, beneficial procedural changes will occur regarding compliance oversight, company policy, and documentation. Staff will begin to realize the importance they play in the organization, and unions will certainly observe the role management is taking with compliance regarding the law and their creation of a safer work environment, especially within the realm of driver fatigue.

➔As the Compliance Coordinator, you're probably beginning to think that you're slightly overwhelmed and that this compliance/cultural thing may be too challenging. Hang in there, because it only becomes more exciting. Regardless of the size of the transit agency, its reputation or the results of previous Terminal inspections and audits, one question is always foremost in the minds of most Maintenance and Transportation Managers and personnel over Pull-Notice and Drug and Alcohol Programs: "If my program is rated Unsatisfactory for whatever reason, will I lose my job?" The challenge with that very sincere question is that few want to discuss it, raise the concern, or initiate a dialog they could regret later.

Typically, at many transits there is generally no company policy or job description that references consequences for an Unsatisfactory Terminal or any other compliance Rating. Among the many things the coordinator must do sooner than later is to work with senior staff and develop clear and definitive language regarding the actions taken, if any, for an Unsatisfactory Rate by the CHP or an official regulatory entity. If and when the language is committed to writing, all responsible parties must be informed of the intent and interpretation of the language. As mentioned earlier in the book, an Unsatisfactory Rating for a public transit manager or director can be devastating and may have serious consequences. Therefore, it is in the best interest of managers and others to reevaluate their compliance program(s), work closely with the Compliance Coordinator or regulatory experts, enlist the continued assistance from the CHP, and apply the recommendations in this book.

➔Last, and possibly most important for the Compliance Coordinator(s), their assistants, or anyone involved with introducing regulatory compliance or making changes to a current program (which is probably not regulatory based), I leave you with this: The task of implementing appropriate vehicle and driver regulations and changing the fabric of the status quo, relative to commercial vehicle law within an agency, sometimes means "pissing people off." Good leadership, from the CEO on down, requires a willingness to make unambiguous choices and difficult (necessary) decisions on the development of a compliance-driven agency, which may require policy change, program modification, and possibly some departmental reorganization.

Attempting to get everyone on board with the new requirements and to accept new processes and procedures will require tenacity, a firm resolve, and a resistance to compromise on what the law mandates. The inspectors even say, "I don't write the law and I can't change it, but I inspect against it." When departments begin to implement legal-based programs and divisions initiate new processes while expecting more accurate records management, and when staff are asked about compliance information by document and title, know that your efforts and those of many others are beginning to take positive effect. Be unyielding, never waiver, and don't compromise, for a compliance culture is being born and the agency will reap the benefits of change.

Fast-Fact Lists

The following reference list is in no specific order of legal or technical importance. The information is available for personal use to facilitate a quick reference of *Title 13 California Code of Regulation*, *Code of Federal Regulations*, *California Vehicle Code*, and the *Commercial Vehicle Safety Alliance Guide* for general use primarily by the public transit operator. The list has been compiled because of frequently asked questions by many transit professionals—mechanics and bus drivers, Maintenance and Transportation Managers, Directors, and other involved personnel—relative to the CHP Terminal inspection, applicable laws and regulations, and numerous bus-related issues.

The list does not constitute a complete statute or regulation, and the user should refer to legal document(s) should more information be required. Further, the CHP Host or assigned MCS I can assist in finding rules and regulations in the various resource documents and are always willing to assist with the interpretation of the language and its intent. And contrary to what some think, the CHP does not write the law and is not authorized to amend, revise, or authorize different language contrary to the reference documents. They do inspect and write violations against commercial vehicle laws and regulations and are authorized to remove buses and BIT vehicles from service for safety-related issues.

If you disagree with a Terminal Rating or an Out-of-Service condition or you simply need clarification on regulatory language, I recommend you discuss the issue with the inspector or the MCS III. If you are not satisfied with the answer(s), you have the right to contact, in writing, the CHP Commissioner, who will respond in writing, generally within 6 weeks. And, no, there will not be repercussions with your decision to contact the Commissioner. Fortune favors the bold, so go for it for the good of your agency, even if it turns out you dislike the response. One thing is certain: You will receive a response, and it will be accurate and concise. *(Note: Secure approval from senior management before communicating with the CHP Commissioner.)*

On a few occasions when I had concerns about an issue, I not only wrote the CHP Commissioner but was encouraged by the inspectors to write; like they told me, "Go ahead. We don't know everything and would also like to read his decision on the issue."

If you decide to correspond with the Commissioner, I suggest you clearly explain your concerns(s) and cite the reference document in question by title and section, as best you understand it. Present your issues and ask for the legal interpretation as it relates to the situation. Again, you'll receive a written response within about 6 weeks.

The Office of the current CHP Commissioner is:

CHP Commissioner
J. A. Farrow
P. O. Box 942898
Sacramento, CA 94298

The following is a fast-fact list by reference document and section.

Title 13, California Code of Regulation

Title 49, Code of Federal Regulations

California Vehicle Code

Transit Bus Driver Certificate...................................§12804.6

Requirement for two-way
    communication device................................§24018

Pull-Notice Program ....§1808.1

Mandatory seat belt law....................................§27315

Bus control and stop requirement.............................§26454

Bus Terminal Inspection,
    Matters Regulated................................§34501 (c)

Terminal inspection, sample size .... §34501.12

Regulated commercial vehicle list..............................§34500

Carrier Identification Number (CA Number).....§34507.6

General Out-of-Service section ....§24002

Education code, Verification of
    Transit Training...§40085.5

CNG fuel compressed or liquefied ....§2402.6

Commercial vehicle PM inspection
    (90-day interval for BIT) ....§34505.5

Drug and alcohol testing.......................................§34520

Bus stopping-distance requirement.........................§26454

License plate display.. §5200

Commercial motor vehicle definition ....§15210

HOV lane use..§21655.5

Vehicle length, bike rack device ....§35400

Use of red warning light..§25269

Deceleration warning lights ....§25251.5 (c)

Commercial Vehicle Safety Alliance Out-of-Service Criteria Handbook and Pictorial

Note: The CVSA is found in 13 CCR §1239 (b).

Driver...Part I, Section 1.

Brake Systems..Part II, Section 1.

Low-Air-Pressure Warning Device ....Part II, Section 1.

Air-Loss Rate ....Part II, Section 1.

Drive Line/Driveshaft ....Part II, Section 4.

Exhaust Systems ....Part II, Section 5.

Frames..Part II, Section 6.

Fuel Systems ....Part II, Section 7.

Steering Mechanisms.....................................Part II, Section 9.

Suspension..Part II, Section 10.

Tires..Part II, Section 11.

Wheels, Rims, and Hubs ....Part II, Section 13.

Windshield Wipers ....Part II, Section 14.

License/Memberships, Training, and Vehicle Stopping Requirements

Inspection and Maintenance Station (IMS) License

A station license issued to a person/agency as cited in 13 CCR, Article 3, beginning in §615, enables fleet owners certain privileges that can only be authorized through the state of California, specifically the *clearance* of vehicle equipment violations from enforcement documents, eliminating the need to take the bus/vehicle into a Highway Patrol office. It is highly recommended that public transit agencies and contract service providers take advantage of the benefits of being IMS certified.

Refer to 13 CCR §617 Procedures for Licensing. Fleet owner inspection and maintenance licensing is issued according to the procedures in this section. For more information regarding IMS certification, contact your MCS or MCS III for details and requirements concerning the display of the license, care of equipment, the enforcement clearance function, and authorized inspection by the Department.

Commercial Vehicle Safety Alliance Membership

The CVSA is an active organization that is committed to support motor vehicle safety and the commercial vehicle operator and to serve as a resource to enact change in legislation, regulations, enforcement, and training for operators. Becoming a member of the CVSA is strongly encouraged and offers many benefits, which include the following:

- The annual updated *North American Standard Out-of-Service Criteria Handbook and Pictorial*
- Listings of conferences, workshops, and training opportunities
- Involvement in working committees
- Education and training material
- Receipt of the quarterly magazine, *Guardian*
- Updates on new or revised laws and regulations that may affect commercial vehicle operators
- Access to experience and knowledge within the commercial vehicle community
- Much more

For information regarding member services, contact *www.cvsa.org.*

CHP Commercial Industry Educational Program

The CHP Motor Carrier Specialists possess a wealth of commercial vehicle information and eagerly offer assistance when contacted. However, they are very busy individuals whose many responsibilities involve motor carrier inspections, evaluations on the effectiveness of maintenance and driver programs, general inspections on many types of commercial vehicles and combinations, bus and BIT inspections, and other required activities. Unfortunately, regulatory training, other than what you can glean from a Terminal, BIT, or administrative review, is not offered through the MCS team. However, the CHP has a training program known as the Commercial Industry Education Program (CIEP). The CIEP offers free educational seminars for carriers and the public transit operator for a wide range of instruction to include:

- The North American Standard Level V inspection
- How to properly perform a Pre-Trip inspection
- Overview of Hours-of-Service regulations
- Drug and Alcohol (check with program coordinator)
- Overview of BIT program

The foregoing list is not exhaustive, and other related training may be offered or designed for your needs. For additional information or to schedule a training seminar or program, contact the CHP, CIEP instructor nearest you:

Northern Division 530.242.4300

Valley Division 916.731.6320

Golden Gate Division 707.648.4180

Central Division 559.453.3100

Coastal Division 805.549.3261

Inland Division 909.806.2400

Southern Division 323.644.9557

Border Division 858.650.3600

Vehicle Stopping-Distance Requirement

Why a stopping requirement? That isn't a law or regulation!

Stop-requirement data for a vehicle is not required by law unless requested by a legal enforcement authority, and stopping-distance calculations are not part of a CHP Terminal audit. However, buses and non-revenue vehicles are involved in crash events; and often regulatory agencies, attorneys, and/or investigative entities need to know, through investigation or discovery, if a "brake and safety" stop test was performed along with a determined stop distance from an initial speed of 20 miles per hour, according to CVC §26454 and CVC §26456. Stop-distance requirements are not part of a Level V Terminal inspection, but this information is provided to you as a necessary resource, as cited within the Vehicle Code, according to the maximum allowable stop distance based on vehicle type and weight. A brake and safety test/inspection for a serious crash event would not be complete without a brake dynamometer test to determine the vehicle's actual stopping-distance performance.

From minor in-service "paint exchange contact" incidents to major crash events, impacts involving transit buses and regulated non-revenue vehicles will inevitably occur, and often the "foundation" or disc brake system is the first thing to be blamed. Following related events, statements of brake fade, grabbing, or no stopping upon brake application are often reported by the driver while in service, by a mechanic on "road test/road call," or by a non-revenue operator. After serious crashes resulting in fatalities or major injuries, a transit agency should immediately perform an in-house "brake and safety" test or contract the activity to a qualified mechanic/brake inspector, assuming there is no legal hold on the vehicle.

To quickly and accurately determine the stopping distance of a vehicle, a portable "on-board" dynamometer should be used. The Vericom (VC 4000DAQ) or equivalent computer accurately measures G Force and calculates speed, time, and stopping distance for all types of vehicles. They are easy to install and operate, self-calibrating, and extremely reliable. Stopping-distance tests for most vehicles can be performed and recorded within 1 hour.

The contact information for the VC 4000DAQ is as follows:

Vericom Computers, Inc.
http://www.vericomcomputers.com

Appendices

Appendix A
Pillars of Regulatory Compliance by Department

The following is a list of required regulatory compliance inspections that each department is responsible for, whether annual or BIT (as requested by CHP). The inspections are required by law; and all managers, department heads, and senior management personnel must be reasonably aware of, if not proficient in, the inspection types, intervals, language of the law, and overall importance of the activities, relative to the business of the agency. These inspections are Rated, while the Pull-Notice and Drug and Alcohol inspection, assuming they are Rated Satisfactory, release programmed state and federal funds.

In the event of a crash, reported injury, or a simple "slip and fall" on a bus, inquiring investigators or legal authorities will seek information as part of their discovery. I cannot overemphasize the importance of the roles of anyone who maintains, operates, or is involved with regulated equipment or the Pull-Notice and Drug and Alcohol Programs.

Maintenance	*Transportation*	*Administration*
Maintenance program	CDL/medical certificate	Pull-Notice Program
CDL/medical certificate	Verification of Transit Training	Drug and Alcohol Program
Maintenance records	Pre-Trip inspection	
Proficiency requirement	Hour-of-Service regulations**	
Pre-Trip inspection	Proficiency requirement	
BIT*	Transportation records	
	Driver logbooks (grid graph)	
	Secondary employment list	
	P-Endorsement	

* Basic Inspection of Terminal (BIT) for non-bus equipment:

- Equipment inspection program by vehicle type
- 90-day inspection requirement/documentation
- Pre-Trip inspection requirement and record maintenance
- CDL/medical certificate

** Driver Hours-of-Service rules and other Matters Regulated:

- 10-hour rule
- 12-hour rule

- 15-hour rule
- 8/80 rule
- Adverse driving condition regulation
- Secondary employment status
- Log book (note exception from the requirement, 13 CCR §1213)

Appendix B
Front Covers of Reference Documents

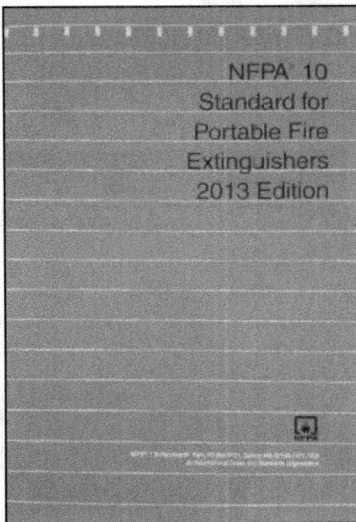

NFPA® 10
Standard for
Portable Fire
Extinguishers
2013 Edition

NFPA® 52
Vehicular Gaseous
Fuel Systems Code
2013 Edition

National Fire Protection Association® 10 Standard for Portable Fire Extinguishers*

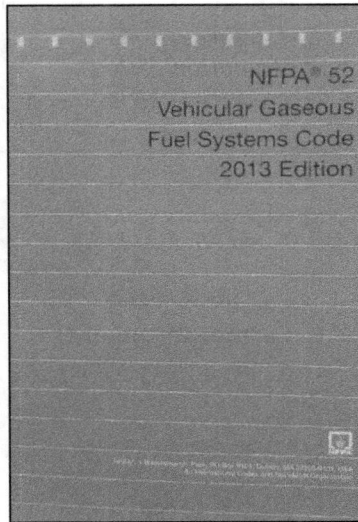

National Fire Protection Association® 52 Vehicular Gaseous Fuel Systems Code*

*© 2013 NFPA. Reproduced with permission.

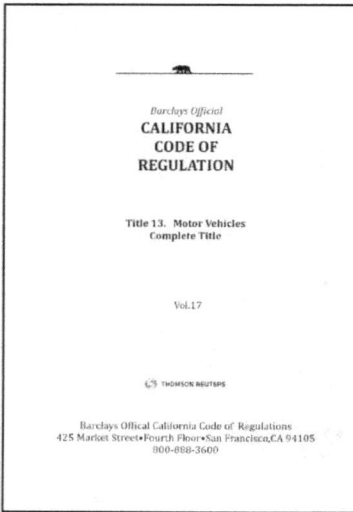

California Code of Regulation, Title 13, Motor Vehicles

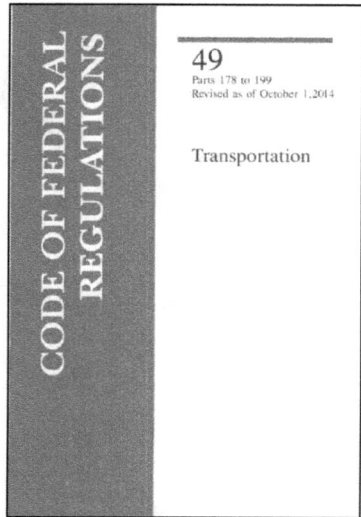

Code of Federal Regulations, Title 49, Transportation

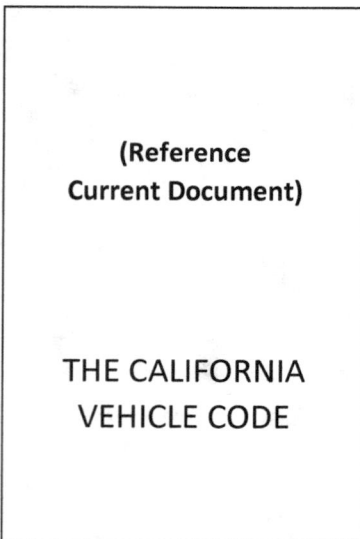

California Vehicle Code

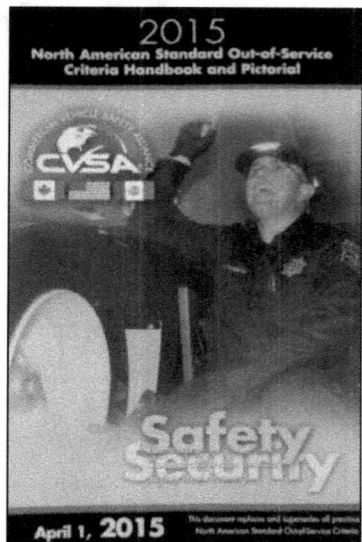

Commercial Vehicle Safety Alliance Out-of-Service Criteria

Appendix C
Records Retention Time Required by CHP Inspectors

Record document	Retention requirement
Bus driver certificate	Not to exceed 5 years
BIT records	2 years/CVC §34505.5 (c)
CHP inspection form (343 form)	4 years at Terminal
Driver license	Until renewed
Driver physical card	2-year update without medical condition, one year with medical condition
Hours-of-Service logbooks	6 months/13 CCR §1234 (a)
Inspection and maintenance repair cards	1 year/13 CCR §1234 (f)
Pre-Trip report*	3 months/13 CCR §1234 (e)

Continued from previous page

Record document	Retention requirement
Pre-Trip repair card	1 year/13 CCR §1234 (f)
Verification of Transit Training (VTT)	Indefinitely
Pull-Notice	Most current record issued
Drug and Alcohol	Current and previous year

---

* Pre-Trip is commonly known as the Driver Vehicle Inspection Report or Card.

Appendix D
Reference Sites and Sources

Analysis and Information
http://ai.fmcsa.dot.gov

California Code of Regulation, Title 13
www.barclaysccr.com/store
http://ccr.oal.ca.gov

California Commercial Driver Handbook
http://dmv.ca.gov
Department of Motor Vehicles
Customer Communications
MS H165
PO Box 932345
Sacramento, CA 94232

California Vehicle Code
http://.dmv.ca.gov

Code of Federal Regulations
http://bookstore.gpo.gov

Commercial Vehicle Safety Alliance, North American Standard Out-of-Service Criteria
http://cvsa.org

Compliance, Safety, Accountability
https://csa.fmcsa.gov

Fatality Analysis Reporting System
http://www.nhtsa.gov/FARS

Federal Highway Administration, Highway Statistics Series
http://www.fhwa.dot.gov/policyinformation/ statistics

Federal Motor Carrier Safety Administration
http://www.fmcsa.dot.gov

Library of Congress
http://loc.gov

National Fire Protection Association— Vehicular Fuels System 52 and Portable Fire Extinguisher 10
http://catalog.nfpa.org

Appendix E
CHP Motor Carrier Safety Unit Locations

Northern Division
2485 Sonoma St.
Redding, CA 96001
530.242.4300

Valley Division
2555 First Ave.
Sacramento, CA 95818
916.731.6300

Golden Gate Division
1551 Benicia Rd.
Vallejo, CA 94591
707.648.4180

Central Division
4771 W. Jacquelyn Ave.
Fresno, CA 93722
559.445.6992

Southern Division
437 N. Vermont Ave.
Los Angeles, CA 90004
323.644.9557

Border Division
9330 Farnham St.
San Diego, CA 92123
858.637.7158

Coastal Division
4115 Broad St., Ste. B-10
San Luis Obispo, CA 93401
805.549.3261

Inland Division
847 E. Brier Dr.
San Bernardino, CA 92408
909.383.4811

Glossary of Common Industry Words, Terms, and Abbreviations

Common Industry Words and Terms

A

Adopted: Laws, regulations, codes, alliances, and any other reference document adopted, means the citing of a reference document by name, title and/or section or edition. For example, 13 CCR has adopted the Commercial Vehicle Out-of-Service Criteria (CVSA) as noted in 13 CCR §1239.

Adverse Driving Condition: As cited in Title 13 §1201 (a) Definition and Title 13 §1212. Driver is authorized to drive for an additional 2 hours, totaling 12-hour drive time, under adverse driving conditions.

B

BIT Inspection: CVC 34501.12 The Basic Inspection of Terminal (BIT) inspection, when required, is performed by the CHP Motor Carrier Unit, primarily to ensure that non-bus-related equipment is safe, repair records are current, and the drivers are legal. BIT equipment does not include buses and is performance based.

Bus: Definition is found in CVC §233.

C

CA Number: Carrier identification number (required). The number shall be displayed on both sides of the bus for every bus in the fleet. The number shall be in contrast to the background and shall be legible during daylight hours from a distance of at least 50 feet. *Authority cited: CVC §34507.6 (b) (1)*

CHP Terminal Inspection: The inspection required of California motor carrier vehicles described in CVC 34501 (c) bus and CVC §34501.12 truck. The inspections include maintenance and driver records, inspection of a representative sample of the equipment, Pull-Notice, and the Drug and Alcohol Program.

Cite the Authority: To request an individual to state in what reference document, by title and section, the issue, statement, requirement, or Out-of-Service condition may be found.

Commercial Vehicle: Definition is found in CVC §260.

Compliant Program: Programs, processes, equipment, record maintenance, and/or procedures required must be compliant with commercial vehicle laws, regulations, alliances, and codes.

Composite Terminal Rating: A Terminal is inspected for either bus or BIT and issued a Rate based on the condition of the vehicles, equipment, and driver records to determine if the carrier is in compliance with commercial vehicle rules and regulations. One composite Rate is issued for the Terminal based on all the inspection criteria.

Compliance: Practice of obeying a rule, regulation, law, code, or agreement.

Crash: Any vehicle(s) involved in physical contact and/or when injury or fatalities have occurred.

D

Data Source: Source for factual information. With regulatory compliance issues relative to equipment inspection, crash investigation or any other compliance information, factual source data information is essential.

Dead Bus: Bus that is unavailable for revenue service because of regulatory compliance issues. Bus shall be rendered compliant before it is legal to operate in service.

Driver: Definition is found in CVC §305.

Driver Proficiency: 13 CCR §1229. The driver must demonstrate familiarity with the controls and specifics of the vehicle and be capable of safely operating the bus or any other commercial vehicle required of driver to operate. The language applies to drivers who possess a CDL (mechanic, bus driver, tow truck operator, parts truck driver, and any other person who operates a commercial vehicle as referenced in CVC §34500).

Driver Records: Terminal inspection shall include, but not be limited to, Pull-Notice Program, driver Proficiency, and timekeeping records.

Driver Vehicle Inspection Report: 13 CCR §1234 (e). Same as Pre-Trip inspection. The driver of a commercial vehicle is required to perform an inspection of the vehicle before operation in service. Inspection shall be documented and the record maintained for at least 3 months by the carrier. Bus pre-trip inspection time varies, but the average in the industry appears to be approximately 10 minutes.

Drug and Alcohol Inspection: See *Code of Federal Regulations, Title 49* Part 382 §382.103 (a), and CVC §34520 (a) and (b), and all sub sections within §34520.

E

Endorsements: CVC §15275 (a) Endorsement is required of a driver operating a commercial vehicle unless otherwise required. See also CVC §15278.

Equipment Hold: Bus or non-revenue (BIT) vehicle is not allowed to enter service until all Out-of-Service repairs are completed.

F

Federal Motor Carrier Safety Regulations: See 49 CFR, Part 300 to 399, Subchapter B.

Fleet Owner Inspection and Maintenance Station (IMS): See 13 CCR §615.

Fouling: Any interference between such components as chaffing hoses, fuel lines, or air lines contacting each other or tires. Electrical wires, harnesses, and connectors in contact with themselves will also be considered fouled.

Many "fouling" instances are considered Out-of-Service violations. Refer to CVSA or contact an MCS or the Division Host for an opinion.

H

Hard Hold: A commercial vehicle is placed Out-of-Service and must not be used in service until all repair(s) are completed.

Host: Most commercial vehicle operators/locations have an MCS I who is consistently assigned. The Host may perform the Terminal inspections or be part of the larger team. Regardless, the Host is the point of contact for all Matters Regulated, inspections, or any other issues relative to commercial vehicle law.

Hours-of-Service Regulations: As cited in 13 CCR §1212 Driver Hours-of-Service, Article 3 General Driving Requirements.

L

Long-Standing Defect: A hard-hold defect that has been a violation for a long period that should have been found on a preventative inspection and repaired. Example: a missing brake block bolt or brake wear deep into the scribe line, or excessive (violation of CVSA) steering free play.

M

Maintenance Manager: Individual responsible for all matters that occur at the Maintenance Department within a public transit agency. (Understandably, not all transits within California refer to the position similarly.)

Maintenance Records: Includes but not limited to all required maintenance, lubrication, equipment repair records, and driver Pre-Trip inspection. Refer to 13 CCR §1234 (f).

Matters Regulated: Legal requirements relative to commercial vehicle law and other regulated requirements.

"Maximum Allowable" Out-of-Service Criteria: Refer to CVSA guide.

Motor Carrier: See CVC §408 for definition.

Motor Carrier Specialist: An individual who works under the Department of the California Highway Patrol and who inspects motor carriers for compliance, evaluates the effectiveness of preventative maintenance programs, and inspects for adequacy of maintenance and transportation records and other Matters Regulated. Also called an MCS.

N

National Fire Protection Association (NFPA 10 and 52): Standards for Portable Fire Extinguishers and Vehicular Fuel Systems Code, respectively.

Non-Revenue Vehicle: Equipment other than a bus that is considered a (BIT) vehicle and cited in CVC §34500.

O

Out-of-Service Violation: A commercial vehicle declared Out-of-Service by any authorized person for a mechanical condition for reasons that could possibly cause a crash or system failure. The Out-of-Service vehicle shall not be operated in service until the violation has been corrected. Refer to CVSA.

P

Pencil Whipping: Submitting work cards, either manually or electronic, for repair and/or service that did not occur.

Pre-Trip Inspection: In 13 CCR §1215 Vehicle Condition, it reads that it is unlawful for a driver to operate a commercial vehicle that is not in safe operating condition.

Preventive Maintenance: Maintenance scheduled typically by mileage.

Pull-Notice Program: A legal system for providing the employer with a report showing, for a driver with a Commercial Driver License, the driver's record, indicating the suspensions, subsequent convictions, failures to appear, accidents, license suspensions, or any other action taken against the driver. Pull-Notice inspections occur at transit agencies annually and are performed by CHP Motor Carrier Inspectors. *Employer Pull-Notice (EPN) is synonymous with Pull-Notice Program (PNP).*

R

Regulated Vehicle: Commercial vehicle, as referenced in CVC 34500.

Relief Vehicles: Typically sedan and small van-type automobiles are used to make driver relief. The vehicles are usually not considered commercial vehicles, since almost none are listed in CVC §34500. As such, all time spent in a relief vehicle is considered on-duty time and not drive time for log-book purposes.

Representative Sample: This is the number of vehicles selected for the CHP Safety Compliance Inspection for bus and BIT.

Required: This means "required" by statutory law, regulation, code, alliance, or other law.

Revenue Vehicle: A public transit bus that generates a revenue for service provided.

S

Safety Compliance Ratings: *Title 13, California Code of Regulation,* §1233 Satisfactory, Unsatisfactory or Conditional Ratings issued by CHP Motor Carrier Specialists. Motor Carrier Terminals are assigned a Rating pursuant to 13 CCR §1233 (a) and §1233 (b) (2). The Rating reflects the Terminal's overall compliance relative to applicable laws and regulations.

Secondary Employment: *Title 13, California Code of Regulation,* §1213 (d) refers to a change of location of duty status. The bus driver must file a log with appropriate entries indicating secondary employment. Motor Carrier Inspectors often request listings of drivers with secondary employment.

Short-Standing Defect: A defect that is considered Out-of-Service yet does not go against the overall Rating of the Terminals program. Examples: A light bulb that does not illuminate because of a burned filament, or a tire with sidewall damage as referenced in CVSA.

Speedometer: This is required equipment based on CVC §24017.

Supremacy Clause: State laws shall meet or exceed federal law. Article VI, §2 of the U. S. Constitution reads: "This Constitution, and the laws of the United States which shall be made in pursuance thereof; and all treaties made, or which shall be made under the authority of the United States, shall be the supreme law of the land; and the judges in every state shall be bound thereby, anything in the Constitution or laws of any state to the contrary notwithstanding."

T

Terminal: A place where a bus or any other vehicle listed in CVC §34500 is maintained, garaged, or dispatched. Also referred to as a depot.

Terminal Re-Inspection: Takes place 120 days after an Unsatisfactory Rating.

The Department: The Department of the California Highway Patrol.

Terminal Compliance Inspection: For this definition, see CVC §34501.12.

Tire Mileage Program: When a public transit agency or a contract service provider is under a tire "mileage" program, all tire service, rubber, and maintenance is provided by the contractor under a mileage rate and a service premium by tires, based on miles driven, typically on a monthly billing cycle. The transit agency does not own the tires or provide tire service (in most instances), and liability is on the program provider. Not only does the program relieve the transit from tire-related liabilities, but the contractor ensures that the tires are properly inflated, "skid tested" (tread depth measurement), inspected, repaired, and replaced on an as-needed basis. The removal and disposal activity of spent tires is performed by the contractor. Most mid- to large-sized public transit agencies and many transit contract service providers are on mileage programs.

The Goodyear Tire and Rubber Company is the leader in mileage programs. For more information about a mileage program with Goodyear, contact 1-800-MILEAGE (800.645.3243).

Transit Bus: Definition is found in CVC §642.

U
Unsafe Vehicle: As cited in CVSA or CVC §24002.

V
Verification of Transit Training: See CVC §40085.5 Education Code (Driver Education and Training). An 8-hour training requirement per year, from birth date to birth date, is required for all transit bus drivers.

Common Industry Abbreviations

A

A&I	Analysis and Information
ABA	American Bus Association
APTA	American Public Transit Association

B

BIT	Basic Inspection of Terminal
BO	"Bad Order" bus that has noted violations or is Out-of-Service

C

C	Carrier
CA No.	Carrier identification number
CARB	California Air Resources Board
CDL	Commercial Driver License
CEO	Chief Executive Officer
CEP	Commercial Enforcement Personnel
CCR	*California Code of Regulation*
CFR	*Code of Federal Regulations*

CHP	California Highway Patrol
CIEP	Commercial Industry Education Program
CIRES	Carrier Information Reporting and Evaluation System, formerly called the MISTER report
CLETS	California Law Enforcement Telecommunication System
CMV	Commercial Motor Vehicle
CNG	Compressed Natural Gas
COO	Chief Operations Officer
CSA	Compliance, Safety and Accountability
CTA	California Transit Association
CVSA	*Commercial Vehicle Safety Alliance*
CVC	*California Vehicle Code*

D

D&A	Drug and Alcohol
DLMS	Driver License Monitoring System
DMV	Department of Motor Vehicles
DOT	Department of Transportation/Federal
DVIR	Driver Vehicle Inspection Report

E

EPN	Employer Pull-Notice (same as Pull-Notice Program, PNP, or the Driver License Monitoring System)

F

FARS	Fatality Analysis and Reporting System
FHWA	Federal Highway Administration

FMCSA   Federal Motor Carrier Safety Administration
FMCSR   Federal Motor Carrier Safety Regulations
FMVSS   Federal Motor Vehicle Safety Standards
FTA   Federal Transit Administration

G

GM   General Manager
GPPV   General Public Para Transit Vehicle
GVW   Gross Vehicle Weight
GVWR   Gross Vehicle Weight Rating

H

HOS   Hours-of-Service
HPG   *Highway Patrol Guide*
HPH   *Highway Patrol Handbook*
HPM   *Highway Patrol Manual*

I

IMS   Inspection and Maintenance Station (License)

J

JADIC   Justice Department Interface Controller

L

LNG   Liquefied Natural Gas

M

MAIT   Multidisciplinary Accident
         Investigation Team

MCMIS	Motor Carrier Management Information System
MCS	Motor Carrier Specialist (I, II, or III)
MKP	Most Knowledgeable Person

N

NFPA	*National Fire Protection Association* (Code or Standard)
NHTSA	National Highway Traffic Safety Administration
NTSB	National Transportation Safety Board

O

OAL	Office of Administrative Law
OOS	Out-of-Service

V

VTT	Verification of Transit Training

P

PM	Preventative Maintenance
PNP	Pull-Notice Program (Same as Employer Pull-Notice)
PSIP	Periodic Smoke Inspection Program

S

SPAB	School Pupil Activity Bus

Acknowledgments

To my life partner and incredible wife, Tawny. Like precision global positioning, you kept me on course, humble, and focused throughout the project. Your assistance was invaluable and timely.

Mike Kelley, Motor Carrier Specialist III (retired) from the CHP Motor Carrier Southern Division, you are the indisputable expert on commercial vehicle law and all Matters Regulated. Without your willingness and patience to explain the regulations to me, this book would not have been written. For over 25 years you have shared your valuable knowledge regarding laws and regulations, the Terminal inspection process, and the complexities of how the regulatory dots are connected. Thank you for your friendship and support.

Gwen, only your artistic mind could have created this fabulous book cover, and the illustrations were spot on! Thank you.

About the Author

Michael L. Stange is a public transportation professional with over 40 years of experience. He began his career as a bus mechanic and retired from the Los Angeles County Metropolitan Transportation Authority as the Executive Director of Maintenance. He has worked closely with the CHP Motor Carrier Specialists and Multidisciplinary Accident Investigation Teams, has assisted in crash investigations, and is an expert in commercial vehicle law for public transit operators. He developed and teaches an 8-hour regulatory compliance program for the transits and also provides the program, when requested, through the Southern California Regional Transit Training Consortium, the leading provider of transit training within the public transportation industry.

He is a recognized expert in regulatory compliance and Terminal inspections for public transit operators, according to the Southern Division, CHP Motor Carrier Team based in Los Angeles. During his career, he has been involved in more than 600 CHP Terminal inspections, Triennial, BIT, Pull-Notice, and Drug and Alcohol audits.

Applying his broad public transportation experience and extensive knowledge of commercial vehicle law, Michael offers professional advice, compliance information, and training to transit personnel located throughout California.